BULLY BEEF AND BOILED SWEETS

BULLY BEEF AND BOILED SWEETS

by
James Mannion

Constable • London

Constable & Robinson Ltd.
55–56 Russell Square
London WC1B 4HP
www.constablerobinson.com

First published in the UK by Constable,
an imprint of Constable & Robinson Ltd., 2013

A copy of the British Library Cataloguing in Publication Data is available
from the British Library

ISBN: 978-1-78033-606-0 (hardback)
ISBN: 978-1-78033-608-4 (ebook)

1 3 5 7 9 10 8 6 4 2

DEDICATION

For Shelley and George for giving me someone to cook for.
I love you.
And for the brave men and women in the British Armed Forces
who do unimaginably hard things, in impossibly difficult situations,
for unquestionably too little praise, every single day of the year in
order to keep us all safe. 'Hero' is too small a word.
From my family and I – 'Thank You'.

CONTENTS

INTRODUCTION

An Army Marches
on its Stomach

It was Napoleon Bonaparte who said, 'An army marches on its stomach.' He may have been short and French, but he was absolutely right. For over three hundred years, the British Armed Forces have been made up of brave men and women who put themselves in harm's way so the rest of us can sleep soundly in our beds. Marching alongside every division, every battalion and every soldier, no matter where in the world they were needed, was the chef, who had to be just as handy with a Browning L9A1 9mm semi-automatic as a whisk and a rolling pin. For they not only fought alongside their fellow troops but also whipped up a hot meal for them when they returned to base.

The importance of that job cannot be overstated because food in the Forces is not just about giving someone a meal. It's about morale, it's about preparing someone for battle and it's about doing all of this with ration packs, very few (if any) fresh ingredients and the very simplest of cooking kit. Yet Forces chefs continually deliver the best possible food in the most trying of conditions – be it a smart reception for high-ranking VIPs in a posh hotel, or for their fellow troops up a snowy mountain or in the deepest, darkest jungle. (And all this despite their comrades-in-arms joking that the chefs' course must be the hardest of all the divisions because no one has passed it in years.) For Forces chefs such tricky circumstances (and gags) are no impediment to producing amazingly tasty, exciting and varied food. The saying goes that 'necessity is the mother of invention' and nowhere is that more true than in the British Forces' catering arm, where each chef must feed hundreds of men a different meal three times a day from the same often limited ingredients.

This then is what *Bully Beef and Boiled Sweets* is all about – a celebration of the skills and achievements of this country's military chefs. You'll discover the meals they serve the brave and selfless men and women who, even now, are putting themselves in dangerous situations so we are free to muck about in the kitchen – and then cook them ourselves. If you haven't done much cooking before, don't worry, this is the perfect book for you. Each recipe is stripped back to be as simple as can be – after all, they are often cooked for hundreds of men and women, with only a handful of ingredients on the most basic cooking equipment. And for those of you who know their way around a blender, I hope you will enjoy the amazing things that these chefs produce from these fundamental foodstuffs and marvel at their inventiveness. (And if you want an even more authentic experience you can always get someone to throw blunt objects at you and drop big pans on the floor whilst you cook to simulate combat conditions.)

> **" Forces chefs continually deliver the best possible food in the most trying of conditions... "**

As well as discovering what troops are fed now you'll also see what has been served up in the major conflicts, from World War I to the present day. You'll learn how to catch, kill and cook your food when stranded in the middle of nowhere and there isn't a kitchen or KFC to be found. You'll see what some of our most famous ex-servicemen enjoyed eating whilst they were in the British Forces; and, finally, what fine foods the officer class get served in contrast to the squaddies.

All the recipes run alongside fact boxes and fascinating food-related bits and bobs that explain just what is in an army ration pack, why eating army food could very well effect erections and why you owe your Friday night chicken tikka masala to the Army. So for anyone who ever pretended a tree branch was a machine gun, who admires what our Forces go through every single day and who wants to improve their kitchen skills, *Bully Beef and Boiled Sweets* is for you.

CHAPTER 1

Bully Beef, Stiff Upper Lips and a Lot of Carrots

The British Army has been involved in its fair share of dust-ups over the last hundred years or so. Success in these conflicts would have been much tougher were it not for the excellent food served to our boys and girls at the front. In this chapter you'll discover what our troops were fed in the major historical conflicts of our time – World War I, World War II and beyond – and learn to cook them for yourself. Be prepared for such wonders as the Woolton Pie, Baby's Head Pudding and the universally beloved Egg Banjo.

WORLD WAR ONE TRENCH STEW

The British Army has always faced extremely tough conditions – circumstances that would have the vast majority of us running home to our mothers. But, arguably, the theatre of conflict during World War I was the most inhospitable of all. Living, fighting and eating in little more than a muddy hole in the ground, things were certainly tough for the humble Tommy at Ypres, Verdun and the Somme. And that's without the nonsensical leadership of stiff-upper-lipped officers ordering them to walk in the face of heavy machine gun fire because to run just 'wasn't cricket'. Sadly, for these put-upon men, the food wasn't going to raise spirits any time soon. For our boys at the front, both the quantity and quality of grub on offer was enough to make them wish for a serious case of trench foot and a return trip home.

The bulk of their diet in the trenches was made up of bully beef (a sort of canned corned beef), bread of varying degrees of edibility (by the winter of 1916, for example, flour was in such short supply that bread was being made with dried, ground turnips), and, er, that was about it. Ever resourceful, though, the hard-working British Army kitchen staff on the front line weren't to be beaten and would liberate – and by 'liberate' we mean 'steal' – vegetables from local farms, as well as use weeds and nettles to improve soups and stews. (Imagine how bad the food must have been for weeds to make it more appetising!) They would also (and fans of *War Horse* should look away now) cut up and cook horse meat from their fallen four-legged comrades.

To add insult to injury, the various battalions' kitchen staff had such limited resources that they had to prepare everything the soldiers ate in the same pots and pans – the result being that everything ended up tasting the same – soldiers would often complain, for example, that their tea tasted of vegetables.

Providing food to our troops was also logistically very difficult. Without the infrastructures that are established in a modern theatre of war as a matter of course, it took up to eight days for

> " Trench Stew ... was a common World War I recipe ... It also tasted pretty good – especially considering the alternative was to starve. "

food to reach the boys on the front line (there were soldiers called 'soup runners' whose sole jobs it was to get the grub to troops as quickly as possible). So food was, at best, stale and, at worst, full of bullet casings, mud and bits of Jerry. The British soldiers – never letting such inconveniences get them down – simply removed such foreign objects, mashed up what was left and got it down them. Many also made attempts to fend for themselves, scavenging what they could before cooking it up over a small stove they had clubbed together to buy or, even, managed with a lit candle.

Trench Stew, then, was a common World War I recipe. It's pretty simple and so a good place with which to start the book and get you into the swing of things. It could be prepared in the field kitchen to be delivered to the Front, or made by the humble Tommy in his mud-filled trench, over his very own candle. It also tasted pretty good – especially considering the alternative was to starve.

For two servings

You will need:
600ml water
salt and pepper
1 turnip
2 carrots
stock cube for flavour (you could 'keep it real' and throw in some nettles and whatever else you can find growing in the gaps between your patio paving stones)
½ x 340g can of corned beef
2 plain biscuits (something suitably dull like a Rich Tea or a plain cream cracker would be the closest match. Actually, the closest match would be a large square dog biscuit but this is not about to be the first cookbook in the world to list a canine treat as a cooking ingredient)

How you do it:

1 First pour the water into a saucepan, throw in a little salt and bring it to the boil. While the water is heating up, peel and slice the turnip and carrots into bite-sized chunks (none of that nouvelle cuisine julienning of veg for the boys in WWI).

2 When the water is merrily bubbling away, chuck in the veg and stock cube (or nettles) and leave them to cook for about 10 minutes. You'll know when the veg are ready when you can stick a fork into them nice and easily but they haven't yet turned to mush. (So, if they are still a bit firm, no drama, just boil for a little longer.)

3 When the carrots and turnips are good to go, chop up the corned beef and add to the mixture and give the lot a really good stir. Heat the meat for a minute or so (you don't want to leave it too much longer as you run the risk of the veg going too soft) and then take the pan off the heat and add in your biscuits, snapped into whatever size portions as takes your fancy. Taste it and add a little salt or pepper if you think it needs it.

4 If you think the stew is still a little watery you can always thicken it up with a tablespoon or two of plain flour, blended with a little water until smooth. Stir it in a little at a time until it is a consistency you are happy with. Let it bubble for a minute or two so it doesn't taste all powdery, and then get stuck in. (If you want complete authenticity, serve the stew in a metal bowl and eat in a pre-dug, six-foot trench filled to waste height with muddy water. Should your partner complain you've ruined the garden, explain you are celebrating the pluck and courage of the British Army, who have done so much to put the 'great' into Great Britain. Do be prepared for at least one week's exile to the spare room or sofa for taking such action – a small price to pay, I'm sure you'll agree.)

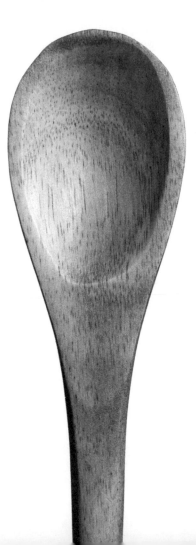

THE FOUNDER OF THE FEAST WAS FRENCH

Not surprisingly with such a book title, this tome is overwhelmingly and unashamedly patriotic. But we are fully aware of the contributions made by foreigners to the British Army story. One towering example of this is the huge debt our army owes to one Alexis Benoist Soyer.

Soyer was a quite remarkable French chef who, in his short life, cooked for princes and prime ministers and invented many of the kitchen staples we now take for granted, like cooking with gas and having ovens with adjustable temperatures. He was also the Jamie Oliver of his day – he wrote numerous cookbooks to show how it was possible to feed your family for very little money (which was lucky because during the Victorian era that's exactly how much most

people had). More relevant to us, though, was his sterling work with the catering arm of the British Army. During the Crimean War, Soyer joined the British troops at the front – at his own expense – and systematically changed the way our Army fed itself. For instance, he trained and installed in every regiment a cook whose responsibility it was to feed the rest, which was a giant leap forward as, until then, it was every man for himself and many suffered and even died from food poisoning and malnutrition. He also designed and built his own portable stove – the Soyer Stove – which soon became essential kit for every section of the Army and meant that troops could prepare food wherever they were. A modernised version of it is still in use today.

On returning from the war, Soyer continued to aid our military by lecturing all over the country on how important it was to improve the cooking standards for serving men. He even got round, in his spare time, to designing, building and installing the kitchens at Wellington Barracks – the building, near Buckingham Palace, which houses the soldiers who guard the royal family to this day. His contributions have not been forgotten and in acknowledging what a huge difference this man made to our boys, the cooking arm of the Army – the Royal Logistic Corp – named their HQ 'Soyer House'.

BULLY BEEF COTTAGE PIE

There are certain words guaranteed to stir the blood of the British gentleman. Slip a mention of 'Jet from *Gladiators*' into the conversation, and men of a certain age from John o' Groats to Land's End will adopt a far-away look in their eye as they recall blissful Saturday evenings past. Similar patriotic responses can be noted when raising such subjects as the romance of the FA Cup third round, bank-holiday weekends, or from humming the opening bars to the 'Dambusters' theme. Well, prepare to add to that esteemed company the foodstuff known as 'Bully Beef', a manly meat that screams of daring deeds and stiff upper lip-itude! It's been an army staple that has seen service from as far back as the 1890s and the Boer War, and helped the British Army win both World War I and its inevitable sequel, World War II – from where this recipe is drawn. (And, by the way, just take another look at the name of the recipe at the top of this page. 'Bully Beef Cottage Pie'. Could there be a more British-sounding meal than that?)

So what exactly is this loyal servant of the Armed Forces – bully beef? Well, it's not quite as mysterious as it sounds. For it is nothing more than common-or-garden corned beef. It's brisket of beef (the breast or lower chest bit of the cow) that is cooked, cured and then packaged in a can. Those etymologists out there – or, to give you your completely unofficial title, 'boffins of word-meaning' – will no doubt already know that 'bully beef' is an anglicised version of the French *Boeuf Bouilli*, which means 'boiled beef' and refers to how the meat was initially prepared. Boiling, curing or packing it with gelatine and stuffing it in a can, were all good ways of keeping the beef edible for longer – very important for soldiers on the battlefield, where fresh meat was hard to come by. The other virtue of bully beef is that it's exceptionally versatile. It can be hashed, thrown into all manner of stews or bakes or, for the tired and desperate private, just chucked between two slices of bread or layered on top of a hard tack biscuit ('hard tack' is another regular WWI and

> **"** . . . our humble corned beef has been a reliable, edible friend for the British Army for over a hundred years . . . **"**

WWII food item with a long shelf life, known not just for its portability but also its ability to chip teeth). Simplest of all, it can even be eaten straight out of the can. However they chose to eat it, our humble corned beef has been a reliable, edible friend for the British Army for over a hundred years . . . Or rather it was. For in 2009, the Ministry of Defence announced that it would no longer be included in soldiers' rations. Like Betamax videos, phones with wires and Arsenal's trophy cabinet, it has sadly found itself surplus to requirement in this modern age. The reason for its sad demise is that what was once most agreeable to scoff in the muddy fields of an inclement Europe, doesn't look so appetising in the stifling 50-degree heat of Afghanistan and Iraq. Shame, really, because this World War II ingredient is really rather tasty, as you will now discover with this recipe for Bully Beef Cottage Pie.

For four servings

You will need:
3 large potatoes
splash of milk
knob of butter (not authentic but nice)
2 carrots
200g fresh or frozen peas (the Forces
   use drained, canned peas)
340g can of corned beef
4 teaspoons of gravy granules
1 onion
a little vegetable or sunflower oil
salt and pepper
chunk of Cheddar (or similar) cheese

How you do it:
1 Peel and chop the potatoes into golf-ball-size pieces. Boil them for about 20 minutes in salted water. Give them the once-over when you get to the 15-minute mark by stabbing them with a fork or knife. If it goes in nice and easily then they are ready, if not boil a bit longer but stop before they go too soft. You want mash, not mush. Fish out the spuds but don't throw away the water – you'll

> **66** Bully Beef, a manly meat that screams of daring deeds and stiff upper lip-itude . . . **99**

use it for the carrots in a bit – and pop the potatoes into another saucepan or a bowl, adding in a splash of milk (and a knob of butter if you like – not good for WWII authenticity but great for taste) and mash them before setting them aside.

2 Next, peel and chop up the carrots fairly small (so they don't take long to cook) and drop them into the boiling potato water (also chuck in the fresh or frozen peas, if using). While they're bubbling away peel and dice the onion and fry in a pan with a little oil until it goes soft and golden brown. Remove the onions from the heat, chop up the corned beef and add it to the onions, and give it all a good mix together. Check the carrots are tender, the same way as for the potatoes.

3 Drain 150ml of the cooking water into a measuring jug and discard the rest. Whisk in the gravy granules until they've dissolved – if it doesn't look thick enough for your liking, throw in another teaspoon or so of granules and mix again until it has the consistency you like.

4 Put the cooked carrots and peas, along with the corned beef and onion, into an ovenproof dish (add the canned peas, if using, at this stage). Next, pour over the lovely thick gravy, and mix it all together before adding a little salt and pepper to taste. Spoon the mashed potato on top of the dish and make sure it covers all the meaty goodness beneath. If you are feeling arty, rough up the mash with a fork to form 'peaks' that will brown nicely. Grate over some cheese and then pop in an oven for about 30 minutes, or until the cheese has melted and gone a golden brown.

REPRO RATIONS

Military re-enactments are a peculiar phenomenon. Populated by men who give up their weekends to run around in muddy fields, playing soldiers and spending fortunes on getting every bit of period kit reproduced as accurately as humanly possible. It's fair to say it's a pastime that's not for everyone. Whether it's recreating Viking broadswords, English Civil War pikes or WWI bolt-action rifles, they take the whole thing very seriously indeed. And thank goodness they do, as it means we can experience exactly what our boys on the front line went through – including what they ate – during WWII.

The excellent Repro Rations website (www.reprorations.com) sells exact reproductions of the ration packs – even down to precise copies of the labels and packaging – that our boys tucked into while fighting off the Bosch, Hun and Jerry. So thorough is the site that you can even buy authentic loo roll – Compo Latrine Paper – which was issued as part of every WWII ration pack. (Serving soldiers were expecting to survive on four sheets of approximately A4-sized paper a day. Doesn't sound like much but from the accompanying pictures on the site, it looks so scratchy and bark-like that you wouldn't want to use any more than was strictly necessary.)

Back to the food, and what's surprising is the amount of stuff that is instantly recognisable – the perfect example being Heinz beans. 'Compo Beans' were made by none other than one Mr H. J. Heinz and, apart from the 'Government Issue' label, they looked and tasted exactly the same as they do today. Similarly, there are tins of Spam, creamy rice pudding and, of course, this being a 'Brit' ration pack, tea (albeit an instant tea, milk and sugar mix with enough ingredients to make 1.75 litres of tea per man). There are also the more unusual but no less authentic items like malt tablets (a roll of chocolate-flavoured sweeties) and 'brown bread' (a one-pound can of sweetened brown bread laced with raisins). What's also interesting is how much in common these twenty-four-hour ration packs have with the ones being used today. For instance, they both come in several different varieties and both contain very similar items. Compare the following list of ingredients in one of the WWII packs with the modern-day equivalent detailed on pages 62–64 and you'll see what I mean.

The 1944 ration pack contained:

1 can of Spam
1 pack of biscuits brown
   (hard bread/crackers)
1 block of chocolate
1 pack of boiled sweets
2 packets of tea mix
1 packet of sweet biscuits
1 pack of instant porridge
2 packets of meat broth
2 packs of chewing gum
matches
4 sheets of loo paper
menu sheet

BABY'S HEAD PUDDING

In terms of least appetising-sounding recipes, this one, we realise, is going to take some beating. For those of you reading this in north-west Blighty, you'll perhaps still call this very British dish by the same name and know it isn't as disgusting as it sounds. But did you know it originated in WWI and within our very own Armed Forces? For the rest of the country, it may surprise the meat-eaters among you that this uninviting-sounding meal is, actually, steak-and-kidney pudding. This is not the first time steak and kidney has been known by the Army by another name – at points past it's also been called John Bull Pudding, a name so British it makes one want to get up and salute. The reason for the 'Baby's Head' name is hotly disputed, so pick your favourite from the following: a) The pudding is cooked or steamed in a bowl and when it's turned out, the resultant suet-covered delicacy looks like the top of a baby's head; b) It's

called a baby's head because of the sunken soft spot on top of the pudding; or c) When immersed in its statutory lake of gravy, the pudding looks like a baby's head emerging from the brown depths. Wherever it came from, the canned, meaty pie it is named after has been a staple of the Army ration pack since WWI, and has been enjoyed hot or cold and eaten directly from the tin, for nearly a hundred years. However, homemade is decidedly better.

As an aside before we launch into this recipe, there is a simpler way to get a similar dish if you don't fancy making the suet pastry. Gently simmer the meat, onion and herbs in water or beef stock with plenty of seasoning for a couple of hours until tender, then thicken it with the flour blended with water. Put the lot in a pie dish, cover it in ready-rolled puff pastry, brush it with some beaten egg and bake it in the oven at 200°C/gas 6 until puffy and golden brown.

For four servings

You will need:

For the filling:
675g beef shin or chuck steak (any steak will do but these are often the cheapest)
225g ox kidney
1 onion
salt and pepper
1 tablespoon chopped fresh thyme or 1 teaspoon dried thyme
2 tablespoons plain flour
150ml beef stock (or water will do if you really can't be bothered to make up the stock)
Worcestershire or soy sauce (optional)
thick gravy, to serve

For the pastry:
400g self-raising flour
200g shredded beef suet
300ml cold water

How you do it:

1 Chop up the steak and kidney into roughly 2.5cm squares, then chuck them in a large bowl with the peeled and chopped onion. For seasoning, add in a good pinch of salt, pepper and the thyme and mix the lot together and put to one side.

2 Now for the pastry, sift the flour into a large bowl and add the suet and a good pinch of salt and some pepper. Mix it all together and then start adding the cold water a little at a time, mixing as you go. Once all the water is in, you should have a soft but not sticky dough. If it's too dry, keep on adding water, a few drops at a time, until it is the right consistency.

3 Next cut off a quarter of it and put to one side to use later for the lid. Roll out the remainder on a lightly floured surface into a rough disc shape that is about 1cm thick, and use this to line a buttered 1-litre pudding basin. All you need do is really press the pastry around the inside of the basin, but try to make sure there is a bit (1cm or so) hanging over the edge when you're finished. If the pastry splits or breaks open, fear not, just treat it like plasticine and break some more off from elsewhere and squidge it in place to repair the tear. You're not trying to win any 'most beautiful pie' competitions here, so don't worry about it. The important thing is not to have any cracks in the lining when you've finished.

4 That done, go back to your bowl full of ingredients and add in the 2 tablespoons of plain flour and toss the lot together. Add the meaty mixture to the pastry-lined basin and then pour in the beef stock or water. It needs to nearly come up to the top of the bowl but not to cover the meat completely. (If you went with the water option, then chuck in some more salt and pepper for seasoning. A splash of Worcestershire or soy sauce or similar wouldn't go a miss either.)

5 Now take the quarter of pastry you put aside earlier and roll it out so it's about the same thickness but a slightly bigger diameter than the top of the basin, and lay it on top. Seal the lid to the lip of pastry hanging over the bowl with a little water – feel free to employ any pinching or squishing method you desire. Now wrap the whole lot in a muslin

> **“** In terms of least appetising-sounding recipes, this one, we realise, is going to take some beating. **”**

cloth. (You can cover with a double thickness of buttered greaseproof paper or foil if you prefer, twisting and folding it under the rim of the basin to secure. It is important that no moisture can get in.) Lower it gently onto an upturned saucer or small plate that's sitting in a large saucepan. Pour boiling water around the basin to come halfway up the side. Pop on the lid and simmer on a low heat for 4 hours. Check back in every so often to top up with more boiling water if need be, as you don't want the pan to boil dry – take it from me, the blackened mess it leaves behind is a swine to get off.

6 When cooked, carefully lift the basin out of the pan, remove the cloth, greaseproof paper or foil and carefully turn it over onto a plate. (If it doesn't come out first go, turn it back the right way and gently slip a round-ended knife down the edges to loosen it and try again.) Cover the whole lot – including pouring a nice reservoir in the soft spot on top of the pudding – in lovely thick gravy and eat. Perfection.

WOOLTON PIE

It's an established fact that 'war is hell'. The term was coined by US general William Tecumseh Sherman, who fought in the United States Civil War. He was, like all army men of the time, the spitting image of Wolverine-era Hugh Jackman, while bearing the stern countenance of a Sir Alex Ferguson who's just been told the staff canteen is all out of chewing gum! Nothing, perhaps, drives this point home better than the horrifying news that for breakfast, lunch and dinner many throughout WWII had nowt to eat but carrots. Much has been written of both the hardships faced by the British troops fighting in Europe, Africa and Asia, and the heroic stoicism faced by those on the home front. However, little can compare to the brutality of their all having to eat more carrots than the entire cast of *Watership Down* could get through. For during World War II, the one vegetable that was in plentiful supply was the orangey fingers Latin scholars know as *Daucus carota*. So widely available were they

> **"The pie was the creation of the head chef of the Savoy hotel and was widely distributed throughout the British Army ..."**

that the humble veg soon got its own cartoon character – the imaginatively titled 'Dr Carrot' who was designed by Walt Disney and encouraged wartime mothers and serving soldiers to use the root vegetable as a substitute for other, more scarce, foodstuffs. Not content with bigging up the carrot's suitability in meals, the Ministry of Food went even further and, under Government sanction, let the UK public into a little secret. They said the reason the RAF had been having huge success against the Luftwaffe in Jerry's increasing number of night-time raids was down to our plucky pilots chowing down on carrots due to their high beta-carotene content – a chemical they said helped improve night vision. So strong was the story that we still hear parents implore their kids to 'eat up your carrots as it will help you see in the dark'. That's codswallop, of course. The real truth of the matter was that the RAF was having more and more success against the German Air force because we had secretly introduced an airborne version of radar that helped track any invading aircraft.

The carrot mountain, meanwhile, meant its introduction into increasingly random and strange-sounding foods such as carrot jam and carrot marmalade. There was even a push to encourage people to make a homemade drink called 'Carrolade', which was carrot juice and grated swede all squeezed together through some stockings (hmmm, tasty!). You'll be grateful to hear we won't be encouraging you to try that (although carrot marmalade and jam have made a comeback in recent years), but I can recommend the far more appetising 'Woolton Pie', named after the Minister of Food, Lord Woolton.

The pie was the creation of the head chef of the Savoy hotel and was widely distributed throughout the British Army (who used processed carrots that had been dehydrated and shipped overseas in sealed metal containers) and the home front, who were introduced to it via recipes printed in all the major wartime newspapers (this one is based on the 'official recipe' printed in *The Times* newspaper in April of 1941). It's a cracking pie that not only allowed the government to use up all those surplus carrots and, subsequently, got people eating more vegetables; it also achieved its great taste without the use of meat. Something we never thought we'd hear ourselves say.

For four servings

You will need:
450g potatoes
450g carrots
450g swede
450g cauliflower
4 spring onions
1 tablespoon oatmeal
pinch of salt and pepper
chopped fresh parsley
knob of butter, melted
gravy, to serve

How you do it:

1 Put aside two medium-sized potatoes (which we'll use for a pie crust later) and then peel and dice the remaining potatoes, carrots and swede and cut the cauliflower into small florets, discarding the thick stump. Finely chop up the spring onions and then throw all the vegetables, the oatmeal and some salt and pepper into a big pan. Pour in just enough water to cover the lot and then boil for 10 minutes, stirring occasionally.

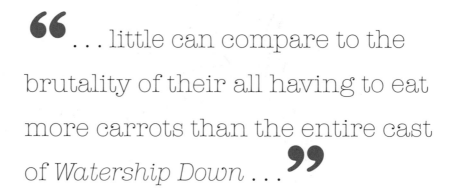

... little can compare to the brutality of their all having to eat more carrots than the entire cast of Watership Down ...

Take the pan off the heat and set it aside to cool for a bit.

2 Next, return to the set-aside spuds and cut them into 5mm thick slices – you are aiming to have enough potato slices to cover the whole of the pie, so cut up another if you feel the need. (The recipe also allowed you to pop a pastry cover on instead if you so desired. Go nuts and try both.) Now drain the cooked veg but reserve the oatmeal cooking water.

3 Preheat the oven to 180°C/gas 4. Put the drained vegetables into a pie dish and then add in just enough of the cooking water to not quite cover them – to prevent it all drying up – and finish the lot off with a sprinkling of chopped parsley. Then cover the pie with the sliced potato (or a pastry duvet). If there is any leftover cooking water, add it to the gravy to serve with the pie.

4 When covered, brush over with a little melted butter and then bake the whole thing in the oven for about 45 minutes or until the potatoes are cooked and have gone a nice golden brown. Take out of the oven and serve covered in lovely hot, brown gravy.

CARROT FUDGE

Whilst carrots played a 'Best Supporting Role' in the previous recipe, here they take centre stage in another WWII cracker. Once again you'll remember that, due to the over-abundance of carrots, they were being dehydrated and shipped to our boys on the European front lines, who were, in turn, using them in loads of grub. This recipe was an attempt to get something sweet into their diet even though sugar was extremely scarce. (It allowed the little they had in ration packs to go a long way, yet could still be cooked even if no sugar were available, as any fruit could be substituted to fairly good effect.)

We grant you that 'Carrot Fudge' sounds weird but, trust us, it tastes good and it must have something going for it as it outlasted rationing and is still served to this day. It's particularly popular in Indian cooking, where a version of it goes by the infinitely more attractive-sounding 'Gajar Barfi'. Enjoy.

Makes about 200g

You will need:

4 heaped tablespoons finely grated carrot
100g sugar (or 100ml orange or apple juice)
1 gelatine leaf, soaked in cold water
a little vegetable or sunflower oil for greasing

How you do it:

1 Put the grated carrot into a pan, pour in just enough water to cover it and simmer gently for 10 minutes or so until it's soft and mushy. Add the sugar (or fruit juice) and stir until the sugar dissolves, then add the softened gelatine leaf. (If you want to go off piste here and go for a less authentic – but, perhaps, more tasty – recipe you can also add condensed milk, butter, vanilla essence or, even, chocolate at this point.) Continue to gently simmer, stirring just enough until the gelatine is completely dissolved.

2 Spoon the lot into an oiled flat dish, and spread it around so the 'fudge' is about 2.5cm thick all over. Put the lot in the fridge for several hours, before cutting into man-sized chunks and scoffing.

ENGLAND v GERMANY

As has been discussed before, physically getting food to soldiers in the two World Wars was extremely difficult. Indeed, when battle was raging (as it was most days) getting fresh food to those at the front was impossible. Soldiers there relied on their ration packs but, when these ran out, would often have no choice after days of near starvation but to retreat from land hard-won from the enemy in order that they could eat.

As Henry John 'Harry' Patch – the man who, until his death in 2009, was not only the oldest man in Europe at the ripe old age of 111 but also our only surviving soldier to have fought in the WWI trenches – recalled in an interview given to Max Arthur for his excellent book *Last Post: The Final Words From Our First World War Soldiers* (Cassell, 2006), 'You were lucky if you got some bully beef and a biscuit you couldn't get your teeth into. If they shelled the supply lines you didn't get anything for days on end.'

However, while it clearly proved very tricky to supply it, theoretically at least our boys at the front enjoyed much better rations than their German counterparts. Records from the time indicate that, on a daily basis, each British soldier should have been supplied with the following: a loaf of bread, some cheese, tea, jam, chocolate and, best of all, a quarter-pint of rum (or a pint of stout if rum was not available) and 20oz of tobacco. Compare this with the German daily allocated ration of just a loaf of bread, some biscuits and 50oz (or in modern speak, about 1.5kg) of potatoes and you can see that poor Jerry didn't stand a chance.

HOMEMADE SAUSAGES

Researching this book has not always been a piece of cake – to use an appropriately foodie term. For instance, in putting together this particular recipe, we had no idea quite what was in store when innocently Googling the terms 'army sausage', 'sausage stuffing' or 'love of sausage'. . . (Thankfully you won't have to stumble across sites that are going to take many years of therapy to forget, for we have done the hard work for you.) What we eventually discovered was that the British Army has been making its own bangers for decades and none other than the esteemed website www.sausagemaking.

org ('the web's favourite resource for sausage makers everywhere') lists this recipe as being an authentic Forces' example from the 1970s. (It comes from the *Manual of Army Catering*, which has been listing snag recipes since the 1950s). Homemade sausages were, therefore, served during the conflicts at Suez, Oman and Northern Ireland, among others. That's a lot of sausage.

This recipe makes sausages how they were – good and fatty. If you want a leaner option, omit the added fat and increase the quantity of meat (but your snags should contain *some* fat or you won't get a good texture or flavour).

> ❝ Homemade sausages were served during the conflicts at Suez, Oman and Northern Ireland, among others. ❞

For four to six servings (about 20 sausages)

You will need:
1.8kg lean stewing beef or pork shoulder (depending on your preference)
900g beef or pork fat
450g breadcrumbs
1½ tablespoons dried mixed herbs
2 teaspoons ground mace
2 teaspoons ground nutmeg
40g salt
½–1 teaspoon pepper
1 litre cold water

How you do it:
1 This is a skinless version of the sausage because a) it's easier and b) it's more authentic. While these days most butchers will sell you sausage casings and you can also buy them online, they weren't, necessarily, readily available in Forces' mess halls throughout the 1950s, 60s and 70s. (Though some examples exist of bangers being made with skins on, goodness only knows what they used – probably best to not think about it.)

2 The most important thing you need to know about making good sausages is that everything needs to be cold. The meat, the fat and even the bowls you'll be mixing in. Doing this will improve the taste and consistency of the finished banger. So pop the meat, fat and bowls into the coldest part of the fridge for at least an hour before you get going. While they are chilling, put the breadcrumbs, mixed herbs, the nutmeg, salt and pepper into a bowl and mix well. Next, pour the cold water into the bowl and leave to stand for 15 minutes in the fridge.

3 Chop the chilled meat in a food processor (not too finely, you still want meaty pieces). If you don't have the kit you can simply chop the meat into 1cm cubes. Then in a chilled bowl cut the fat into roughly same-sized chunks (1cm cubes) and add the coarsely chopped meat before mixing the two together with your hands (move quickly to avoid frostbite). Next, quickly add in the contents of the spiced breadcrumb bowl and mix the lot together before putting it all back into the fridge for 30 minutes.

4 After half an hour has passed, finely chop the mixture in the food processor or pass it through a coarse mincer, or very finely chop by hand (though I don't recommend the third option – jolly hard work). This will be the texture of the finished bangers, so keep going until you're happy with it. When it's ready, on to the final stage – shaping the sausages.

5 First preheat the oven to 180°C/gas 4. Grab handfuls of the mixture and tightly roll it into the classic sausage shape and when all the mixture is gone (you should have enough for approximately 20 bangers), cook the lot in the oven for 20 minutes, turning at the halfway mark to ensure the snags are cooked all the way through. Serve in buns, with mash, or eat off a fork Desperate Dan-style.

IT'S A DANGEROUS JOB BUT SOMEONE'S GOT TO DO IT

Gordon Ramsay may bang on about how hard it is to be a Michelin-starred chef, but plying your trade in a fancy Parisian restaurant is nothing compared with the kinds of dangerous situations Forces cooks have often found themselves in down the years.

Here are but three examples of the courageous escapades of the men in aprons:

- At the first Battle of Ypres in 1915, the German Army very nearly broke through the allied line completely. The only thing that stopped them was a company of 100 cooks, some of whom were only armed with ladles.

- In the Anglo-Zulu war of the late 1870s, during the battle made famous by Michael Caine in the movie *Zulu*, the Company's cook Private Hook held off hundreds of enemy warriors single-handed to protect the injured and sick men in the Company's hospital. His actions earned him the Victoria Cross.

- Cooking on the front line was an especially dangerous thing to do – smoke from the Army ovens would often attract enemy fire and cooks were some of the last British soldiers killed on Armistice Day – 11 November 1918.

EGG BANJO

We humans love a good mystery. What's really stored in the hangars of Area 51? Was Jack the Ripper really Queen Victoria's personal physician sent on a royally sanctioned killing spree? And why do Simon Cowell's trousers start an inch below his nipples? The British Army also has its own secrets. Its soldiers have enjoyed a dish for over 160 years that we have never heard of. One that is cherished by all who come across it and that goes by the peculiar title of 'Egg Banjo' – but just what the heck is it?

By far the greatest weight of evidence suggests the Egg Banjo began life as far back as the 1850s and the days of the Raj, when battalions of the British Army were permanently stationed out in India. The 'Banjo' then followed our boys to the Boer War in South Africa and then on throughout the two big World Wars. The author of the *Flashman* series of books, George MacDonald Fraser, who served in the Army in India during WWII, writes in his autobiography that he remembers

> "... wherever in the world our brave men and women have been sent to serve ... there would be the Egg Banjo offering morale-boosting support."

the 'charwallahs' – Indian civilians who made a living providing all the little home comforts for the soldiers – offering up Egg Banjos alongside mugs of tea and haircuts. Accounts of SAS operations in the 1950s and 1960s out in Far Eastern countries like Malaysia and Borneo also tell of the ever-present Egg Banjo, while closer to home and closer in time, soldiers recount tours of duty in 1970s Cyprus and 80s Northern Ireland, where blissful moments were

spent with the dish. Bringing us right up to date, the Egg Banjo also saw service during the Falklands War, the First Gulf War and is still present and correct during today's engagements in Afghanistan and Iraq. Whenever there has been conflict, wherever in the world our brave men and women have been sent to serve and whatever Division they found themselves in, there would be the Egg Banjo offering morale-boosting support. So universally popular is it, in fact, that it has its own army-generated Facebook page (www.facebook.com/pages/I-love-Egg-Banjos if you are so inclined).

So what is this essential bit of British Army fodder? Well, we shall hold you in suspense no longer. This beloved foodstuff, this vital cog in the military machine, this bit of kit that's as important to the squaddie as his gun, helmet and backpack is none other than the humble fried-egg sarnie. Yes the time-honoured marriage of egg and bread is what has kept our boys and girls going while serving on every continent on the planet.

'That's all very well and good,' we hear you cry, 'but where the heck does that strange name come from?' Well, to understand that you need to imagine the following scene: You're a private returning to base after a long, hard day on tour. It's dark, it's late and it's freezing cold. You dump your heavy kit and trudge to the mess hall for a bit of life-saving sustenance. Stacked high behind the canteen's perspex serving area, still steaming from their time in the frying pan, is a pile of Egg Banjos. You grab one and a mug of tea and take it over to the nearby tables and chairs. You slowly unwrap the warm, tin-foil-encased sarnie, pause a moment while your eyes drink in its yellow and white beauty, and then you sink your teeth right in. At which point, the yolk explodes in your mouth and goes all over the front of your jacket. You jump up, usually uttering the Anglo-Saxon invective of your choice, holding the remainder of the roll high in the air in one hand, while the other rubs up and down your top in an attempt to clear the mess. To all available onlookers – in between fits of laughter – it looks as if you are playing a very tiny air guitar or, more appropriately, banjo – an Egg Banjo.

For one serving

You will need:
old T-shirt or shirt
vegetable or sunflower oil for frying
1 large egg (to use a little military terminology, you want one that is, ideally, the size of a hand grenade. The amount of resultant destruction will be similar)
2 slices of white bread or a white bread roll
butter (or margarine) for spreading
condiments of your choice

How you do it:
1   Firstly, for obvious reasons, put on the old T-shirt or shirt. Then pour a little oil in a frying pan on a high heat to get it nice and warm. While it's heating up, butter the bread, or split and butter the roll.

2   Now the next bit depends on preference. If you like your finished fried egg to have crusty burnt edges, leave the heat up high. If you like your egg to be all smooth and white then turn the heat right down. Crack the egg on the side of the pan and gently open out the shell halves with your thumbs and let the egg slip gently into the oil. (You don't want to rush this bit as a broken yolk will mean you don't get a 'true' Egg Banjo.) Small tip here – if some egg shell falls in the pan when you are cracking it, use the remainder of the shell to fish it out. We don't know why there is such a strange eggy magnetism between the two bits of shell, but we do know it's much easier than trying to do it with a fork or spoon. If you aren't confident about cracking the egg this way, break it into a cup or mug first and then tip it into the pan. Fry the egg, using a teaspoon or spatula to coat the yolky side in hot oil to ensure it cooks too. (You can, once the underside is cooked, take the pan off the heat completely and gently flip the egg over in the oil for a few seconds to cook the other side. This is, however, Advanced Egg Frying, as you risk bursting the yolk and overcooking it – both of which will ensure your Banjo won't play.)

3 Once cooked, remove with a fish slice or spatula and slide on top of one of the bread slices or the bottom half of the roll. Add a dollop of the sauce of your choice – red or brown being most traditional but some have been known to add in Worcestershire sauce or mustard or similar. Whatever floats your boat and makes for a soon-to-be colourful explosion. Gently (you don't want it to go off early) place the other slice of bread or half of roll to the top of your Banjo and then – without cutting, for that would ruin the effect – take as large a bite as you can manage, look down and let the Banjo strumming begin.

CHAPTER 2

Unrivalled Ingenuity, International Cuisine and Spam

Bringing things right up to date, you'll discover in this chapter how the Armed Forces, with the same basic ration packs, serve internationally inspired dishes. There are recipes for British dishes like Chicken and Vegetable Pie, as well as Indonesian Nasi Goreng, Italian Calzone, Mexican Fajitas, Indian Biryani and, of course, this being the Army, more ways to cook Spam than you thought humanly possible.

THE BASICS

Let's start at the beginning. Our troops today, wherever they find themselves in the world, are fed in a whole host of different ways. For instance, they get sent grub from home, they can buy it from the NAAFI (Navy, Army and Air Force Institutes) shops on base and they get given individual ration packs to see them through the times when they are out on operation. (These twenty-four-hour packs are covered in more detail on pages 62–64.) But by far and away the most common method of getting hold of some good 'scran' is through the hard work of a chef from the Royal Logistic Corps cooking for them in a main base mess hall or in one of the smaller forward operating bases (FOBs) using a Vestey Ten Man Ration Pack. The Vestey Group – a British company of over hundred years' experience in the food business – supplies the British Forces with these multiple rations packs that each contain enough food for ten active adults. Each ration contains over 4,000 calories per soldier per day – almost twice what we civvies are recommended to take on board.

The packs come in five different varieties – imaginatively titled Menu Box A, B, C, D and, you guessed it, E – each containing different ingredients to keep meals fresh, varied and exciting. Additionally, each pack can be prepared by a company chef even if he only has access to rudimentary cooking gear and water, which is handy when you find yourself in a war zone. While this perhaps, on paper, doesn't sound like the best starting point for appetising grub, what the modern-day Army cooks do with these ingredients is, quite simply, breathtaking. The entirely different dishes they come up with from, essentially, the same basic building blocks are testament to the level of training and inspired improvisation that is standard in today's Forces.

Each of the following twenty recipes is cooked right now for our troops on active service and all are prepared from the same basic ration packs. So if they can do it in the sweltering heat of a desert, with the very real chance of bullets or bombs interrupting the peeling and chopping, then you can certainly do it at home in the safety of your nice, warm kitchen.

Let's go to work . . .

CHICKEN AND VEGETABLE PIE

As we said in the intro, with the limited nature of the ingredients our Forces chefs have to deal with, it's simply amazing the sheer variety they squeeze out of the ration packs. These next two recipes are great examples of that. They are both made from the ingredients in Menu Box A and yet two more different styles of grub you couldn't imagine. The first is your classic, British comfort food – a Chicken and Vegetable Pie, while the other is a fancy Indonesian dish that wouldn't be out of place on an upmarket Asian menu. It just goes to show the initiative and guile of Armed Forces chefs.

As these are designed to be prepared and cooked in a war zone, they can both be pulled off with just basic cooking equipment, some water and a little bit of confidence (imagine you've just stormed the beaches of Normandy if that helps), so these are a good starting point for the more novice chefs among you. While we stand by what we said in Chapter 1 – that life is too short to bother making your own pastry (and the ready-to-roll varieties that are available today are pretty damn good) – we feel we'd be cheating you if we didn't give you the option of making your own as the Army chefs always do.

> " ... designed to be prepared in a war zone [these recipes] can be pulled off with just basic cooking equipment, some water and a little bit of confidence. "

For four servings

You will need:

For the pastry:
125g plain flour
75g margarine, cut in pieces (other
  cookbooks and your mum would tell
  you that you can use butter – and you
  can – but to be authentic army grub
  you need to do what they do and
  they use margarine because butter is
  harder to come by in Iraq)
pinch of salt
pinch of pepper
splash of cold water

For the filling:
8 bacon rashers (for authenticity the
  ration packs contain Bacon Grill,
  which is chopped and cured pork
  and chicken that comes in a can.
  It's a bit like corned beef but more
  'piggy'. Again, if you are aiming
  for complete authenticity and can't
  get Bacon Grill, just use a can of
  Spam as an alternative)

a little olive oil
3 onions, chopped (the Forces use
  rehydrated dried onion)
400g can of chicken in white
  sauce
300g can of sliced carrots,
  drained
300g can of garden peas
1kg potatoes or mashed potato mix
  (we've made real mashed potatoes
  for the top of the pie, but for a
  closer match to what the Army
  provides, buy a large pack of
  instant mashed potato)
splash of milk
margarine (or butter – again not
  authentic but it tastes nicer)

How you do it:

1   To make your own pastry, sift the
flour into a bowl along with the salt
and pepper. Add the marge and lightly
massage it in with the flour using your
fingertips and thumbs (you will get messy)
until it looks like breadcrumbs. Next, add
cold water a little bit at a time. You want

just enough to bind the dough together,
so stop when you get to that point. It
needs to be roughly the consistency of
plasticine, so if you need more water
splash a bit more in until you are there.
Then dump the dough out onto the work
surface, lightly dusted with some flour so
the mixture doesn't stick to it. (If you are
using ready-to-roll pastry, jump in here.)
2   Roll the pastry out using a flour-dusted
rolling pin until it's roughly the thickness
of a pound coin. Don't worry if it splits
or rips, just tear a bit from the edges and
squish it over the hole. When it's ready
carefully peel it off and use it to line a pie
or flan dish or any similar shallow baking
container, 20–23cm diameter. (Again
don't swear if it tears – it probably will
the first few times you do it – just patch
and mend as you go.) Once you've lined
the bottom and sides of the dish put it to
one side.
3   Cut the bacon (or Bacon Grill or
Spam) into small pieces and fry in a
splash of olive oil until cooked through,
then remove from the pan with a
slotted spoon and put in a bowl. Fry

the onion until lightly browned, then tip it into the bacon.

4 Next, scoop the chicken in sauce out of the can into the bacon and onions, and add the drained carrots and peas. Give it all a good mix and add a little salt and pepper to suit your taste. Carefully spoon the mixture into the pastry-lined pie dish.

5 Finally, make the mash to top the pie. If you are using a packet variety then just follow the instructions. If you are doing this from scratch for the first time then it's really simple. Peel the spuds and chop them up into pieces roughly the size of golf balls (any bigger and they will take longer to cook). Chuck them into a pan of salted water, bring up to the boil and let them bubble along for about 20 minutes. Check them from the 15-minute mark by sticking a fork or knife into one: if it goes in easily they are ready, if not leave to boil for a little longer. When they are good to go, drain them in a colander and return the spuds to the pan, where you can add a splash of milk and margarine or butter and give them a good bash with a masher.

6 Preheat the oven to 180°C/gas 4. Spoon the prepared mash on top of the pie and smooth it out with the back of a fork to ensure it covers the lot. Drizzle over some melted margarine or butter before popping the lot into an oven for 40 minutes until it's all golden brown on top.

NASI GORENG

To just make the point again (as it bears repeating), the same basic ration pack that contained the ingredients that made the classically comforting Chicken and Vegetable Pie on page 37 also has enough in it to make this fancy-sounding Indonesian fried rice dish. As annoying teen speak would have it, 'ZOMG! Totes amazeballs!'

For four servings

You will need:
1 mug of long-grain rice
salt and pepper
margarine
4 sausages, cut into chunks
2 onions, chopped
8 bacon rashers, cut in pieces (again our old friend Bacon Grill is used by the Forces. By all means have it if you can get your hands on some, or try a can of Spam if you want to get a closer substitution)

400g can of red kidney beans, drained
400g can of chopped tomatoes (the Army uses powdered tomato)
1 teaspoon chilli powder
1 egg (again, for authenticity you can use powdered egg as the Army rations dictate. If you do use this classic ingredient, it also has the added bonus of allowing you to pretend to be your gran in war time – pinny and hair rollers optional)
a little vegetable or sunflower oil
soy sauce (optional)

How you do it:
1 Throw the rice into a pan of boiling, salted water and cook for 10 minutes or whatever the packet says. Once it tastes right to you, drain the rice in a colander and rinse with some boiling water from the kettle to remove the excess starch, which keep the grains nice and fluffy and separate. Put it to one side.
2 Then in a frying pan heat up a large knob of margarine (you can use oil, of

course, but marge is what the Army uses) and fry the chopped-up sausages, the peeled and chopped onions and the bacon (or cut up Spam or bacon grill). When the sausages are cooked (no pink bits – cut them open to check), add in the drained kidney beans, chopped tomatoes, chilli powder (more if you like it very spicy but be careful: it will already be pretty fiery) and the boiled rice. Add some salt and pepper to taste, give it a good stir and cook on a low heat for 5–6 minutes or until piping hot. Keep it moving a lot so that the rice doesn't stick to the bottom of the pan and burn. (There's nothing worse than some burnt rice to scupper any dish.) When that's done, take it off the heat, cover it with a lid to keep warm while you prepare the omelette strips.

3 Break the egg into a bowl and whisk it with a splash of cold water and add a knob of margarine (again, you could use milk and butter but this is the way the Army do it). Pour the mixture into a very hot non-stick frying pan (as hot as you dare go) that's been coated with some

oil. As soon as the egg hits the pan, turn the heat down a wee bit and cook for a couple of minutes (you won't need any more). Push the egg about so any uncooked mixture gets its time on the pan and keep going until the egg mixture is set and lightly golden. (Congratulations, you have also just made a basic

omelette, if you've never done one before.) Next, turn it out onto a plate and cut into slices.

4 Mix the shredded omelette in with the hot rice mixture, add a little salt and pepper (and/or soy sauce if you have it) to match your tastebuds and tuck into your Nasi Goreng.

> 66 … for authenticity you can use powdered egg … it also has the added bonus of allowing you to pretend to be your gran in war time – pinny and hair rollers optional. 99

FAST-FOOD NATION

While we are, rightly, concentrating on the meals that are freshly prepared for our troops, as we suggested in the intro to this chapter, that's not the only way serving soldiers can fill their stomachs. It might surprise you to find out that, on main bases like Bastion and Kandahar, the likes of Burger King, KFC, Pizza Hut, T.G.I. Friday's and, most recently, Greggs, all have restaurants, serving the exact same grub they sell on the highways and byways of this fair nation. The idea of having war-zone fast-food joints came – not surprisingly – from our American brothers and sisters, but it was one that we soon nicked and franchises subsequently started popping up on our bases too.

The restaurants are very popular and most soldiers grab a bite to eat there on a regular basis, even though they have to pay for it (food served by the Army chefs is free), and the fast food isn't 'fast' – they often have to queue for an hour to get served. The question then is, 'Why?' Most do it to simply get a taste of home, some for the novelty of doing something 'different', while others draw comfort from it – often going the night before an operation they believe may be dangerous.

So while it may seem a bit weird for us that they are able to order fast food in the middle of a war zone, for those based there, a Big Mac is clearly so much more than just a burger.

> **"** … a Big Mac is clearly so much more than just a burger. **"**

CHOCOLATE FRUIT AND NUT CAKE

A crackling fire roaring in the hearth, the smell of freshly mown grass on a warm summer's morning or the first ice-cold pint supped in your favourite beer garden. Deep down we humans are creatures of comfort and our lady and gentleman soldiers are no exception. How else to explain this very popular – and extremely tasty – sweet treat? It's unbelievably easy to make and will keep even the sweetest tooth satisfied. These are made from the ingredients in Menu Box B.

For four to eight servings

You will need:
200g porridge oats
150ml milk, warmed
200g dried fruit and nut mix
600g sponge cake, cut in cubes
200g jam (any flavour)
200g plain chocolate
a little vegetable or sunflower oil,
   or melted butter

How you do it:

1   First soak the porridge oats in warm milk for a few minutes until they are nice and soft, then drain off any excess liquid and pop them into a mixer (or a big pan and prepare to attack it with a wooden spoon for those of you who don't have the appropriate kitchen gadget).

2   Next, to the oats add the fruit and nut mix, ideally giving the nuts a bit of a bash to break them up before chucking them in. Then pop in the sponge and your preferred flavour of jam. Give it a good mix-up and pop to one side.

3   Now melt the chocolate. You can of course just bung it in the microwave and zap for a few seconds, stir and repeat until melted. This will work just fine but does run the risk of burning some of the choc, which leaves a really bitter taste to the concoction, and a very nasty acrid smell lingering in the air. Better instead to melt it over a bain-marie. (Which is the French way of saying 'pan of simmering water'.) The reason for doing it this way is that the choc will melt slowly, smoothly and won't burn or separate. For a successful water bath, you need a saucepan quarter-filled with water and put on the boil. Then, when boiling, turn it down to a simmer. Sit a heatproof bowl containing the broken-up chocolate over this pan (the bottom of the bowl shouldn't touch the water). Stir at regular intervals to speed up the melt. Once the chocolate is melted, add it to the bowl of mixed ingredients and stir through again.

4   Final leg now: line a sandwich cake tin or shallow baking tin with foil – making sure the foil gets pushed into all the corners and edges. Brush the foil over with a little oil or melted butter. Spoon the mix into the tin and push down well with the back of a spoon, making sure the gooey mess goes into every corner and fills up all available space. Ideally, you will finish with a uniform depth across the whole tin so it 'sets' evenly. Cover the tin with another layer of foil and pop in the fridge for about 2 hours before cutting up into appropriate-sized slabs for your hunger levels, and scoff with abandon.

CHOCOLATE FLAPJACK

When one thinks of traditionally British grub – the kind of stuff that stirs the soul as well as fills the belly – one's mind is soon filled with images of Sunday roast beef with all the trimmings, steaming hot fish and chips and diet-botheringly stodgy, sticky toffee pudding. What, perhaps, doesn't swirl into the brain in quite the same way is the humble flapjack. Well, we're here to tell you that it jolly well should. None other than the world's greatest playwright and proud Brit,

Will Shakespeare, banged on about how great they were way back in the early 1600s when he wrote about them in his play, *Pericles, Prince of Tyre*. Yes we know you've never heard of it, neither had we, but right there in Act 2, Scene 1, he states, 'We'll have flesh for holidays, fish for fasting days and more o'er puddings and flapjacks, and thou shalt be welcome.' And what would be more welcoming on a wet Wednesday while out on operations than a slab of flapjack? Reason enough for our Armed Forces

to regularly knock up a batch of the crunchy yet chewy, sugary treat from the ingredients of Menu Box C. That, and the fact the flapjack is sturdy enough to be swathed in cellophane, stuffed in a pocket and marched through a marsh or sand storm.

" . . . what would be more welcoming on a wet Wednesday while out on operations than a slab of flapjack? "

For four servings

You will need:
150ml water
300g caster sugar
100g margarine
200g porridge oats
100g mixed dried fruit
150g plain chocolate

How you do it:
1 You have to start by making some liquid napalm. No, really, the recipe begins by knocking up some caramel and this stuff is really quite dangerous, so be on your guard. Hi-viz vest on and local emergency services alerted? Then let's begin. Pour the water into a deep saucepan – ideally one that is stainless

steel or has a white bottom to it as this will mean you see the colour of the liquid change as it becomes caramel. Pop it on a low heat and then sprinkle in the sugar and watch it slowly dissolve as you give it the occasional stir. Slowly increase the heat and bring the liquid to a simmer and you will see it slowly thicken into a syrup and, after about 15 minutes, start to brown. It is at this point that you have your semi-deadly sugar-based weapon. Being serious, though, sugar melts at a much higher temperature than boiling water and this sticky liquid will burn and keep burning if it gets on your skin. So be careful, make sure there are no kids or pets running around and all will be well. Another few minutes of simmering and the caramel should be a nice deep amber colour. But don't continue as it will blacken and burn.

2 Take it off the heat and sit the pan in a couple of centimetres of cold water in your sink to stop the caramel cooking further and burning. When it's cooled a little, stir in the margarine until it's melted, then the oats and dried fruit and carefully tip into a greased, shallow baking tin, biscuit tin or similar container. While this is hardening in the tin, melt the chocolate in a bain-marie (for the 'How To' have a gander at page 43 where we used it while making the Chocolate Fruit and Nut Cake).

3 When the chocolate is ready to go, pour slowly on top of the cooling flapjack, spreading it all over with a knife. Leave it to cool, then chill in the fridge for a few hours to firm up before cutting into neat soldiers (or break bits off willy-nilly, whichever is more your style). Either way they're delicious.

BEEF BIRYANI

As if the Armed Forces couldn't get any more awesome, they are also responsible for inventing the Great British Curry. (Don't believe us? See Chapter 5, page 166). So it's no surprise to see a number of these ever-popular dishes regularly being served up in mess halls around the world.

Biryani is a great little curry and differs from most other Indian dishes in two ways. Firstly, it involves a whole heap of vegetables (literally anything you have lying around can go in) and, secondly, the dish has the rice and sauce combined in layers – one layer of rice, one layer of sauce, one layer of rice and so on – before baking through, so all the flavours mix together in one tasty mess. We are going to share two different versions of this dish – one which most accurately follows the sort of thing the Forces would serve, which is, essentially, an assembly job of ingredients. (Nowt wrong with that, nice and quick and very, very tasty.) And then one which is, at heart, the same dish but involves a wee bit more cooking and is a wee bit more complicated. Think of it like playing Call of Duty on 'easy' or 'advanced' mode – the choice is yours. This is made using the ingredients in Menu Box A.

> ❝ As if the Armed Forces couldn't get any more awesome, they are also responsible for inventing the Great British Curry. ❞

'EASY MODE' BIRYANI

For four servings

You will need:
400g basmati (or other long-grain) rice
1 large onion (the Forces use rehydrated dried onion)
400g can of stewed steak
1 small (165g) jar of balti paste
300g can of garden peas
300g can of sliced carrots
salt and pepper

How you do it:
1 Cook the rice per the instructions on the packet. (Usually boil up some salted water, chuck in the rice – 100g or so per person – and then let it simmer away for 10 minutes or according to packet directions. Fish a few out on a fork when you hit that time mark and give them a nibble to make sure they are up to scratch.) When it's done, drain it in a colander and leave over the saucepan, covered with a lid, while you do the onions.

2 As with a number of recipes in this book you can adhere to the Forces method and use dried onions that need soaking to bring back to life, or you can peel, chop and fry a fresh one – the choice is yours. Once that's done, heat the stewed steak (it comes precooked and canned as we're following the Forces way) and mix it with the Balti paste (you can use a curry sauce of course, but they can sometimes be bland and watery and, at best, hit-and-miss, while pastes tend to be nice and concentrated in their flavours). Next, add the drained canned peas and carrots and, finally, the prepared onions from earlier. (Again, for a slightly fresher take on this you can use lightly boiled fresh or frozen peas and peeled, chopped and boiled fresh carrots.) Once this is all mixed together and heated through, begin the layering. In an ovenproof pie dish, start with a layer of cooked rice before adding a layer of meat and veg and then a layer of rice and so on, until the dish is full. Cover with foil and pop the whole lot in a preheated oven at 160°C/gas 3 and heat through for 40 minutes, so that all the flavours can mix and mingle together and it's piping hot before serving. (Be prepared to keep an eye on the dish to make sure it doesn't dry out – if it looks like it is, add a tablespoon or two of water and carry on.) Check that it is cooked through by putting a knife down through the centre, hold five seconds, then remove. If the blade feels searingly hot, it's done; if not, put back for a bit longer.

'ADVANCED MODE' BIRYANI

For four servings

You will need:

splash of olive oil
2 large onions, chopped
1 garlic clove, finely chopped or crushed
450g lean braising steak
165g jar of curry paste
400g can of chopped tomatoes
450ml beef stock, made with 1 stock
    cube
1 large potato, peeled and diced
2 carrots, peeled and chopped
300g can of garden peas, drained
    (or 175g thawed, frozen peas)
400g basmati (or other long-grain) rice
1 teaspoon ground turmeric
salt and pepper
small handful of fresh coriander, chopped

How you do it:

1 Advanced Mode starts with the sauce. On a low heat, pop a splash of olive oil in a large pan and then add the onion and garlic. (It's an extra bit of kit, but for a couple of quid a garlic press will save you a lot of hassle and time in the long run.) Keep the heat low and you'll ensure the onions turn out golden brown and tasty, and you won't burn the garlic, either – this should take 7–8 minutes.

2 While that's sizzling away, cut up the steak into rough 1cm cubes (you don't have to be exact) and when the onions are done, pop the meat in the pan. Keep moving the beef around until it browns and then add in the jar of curry paste, (any will do – balti, tikka masala, rogan josh – though try to avoid korma as it is too mild and this should have a bit of a 'kick'), the chopped tomatoes and the beef stock. Mix it all together again and then pop a lid on the saucepan, turn the heat right down and let it blip away for 1 hour.

3 When the time is up, add the potato, and the carrots. Re-cover and simmer gently for a further 30 minutes. (If the dish is looking dry, add a little boiling water from the kettle to keep it moist), then stir in the peas.

4 While the curry is cooking, do the rice. Bring a pan of salted water to the boil, add the rice and let it cook for 10 minutes or according to packet directions. Test a few grains to make sure it's cooked before draining it, then sprinkle over the turmeric and stir it through. This will turn the rice a lovely yellow colour and add a little more taste and bite. (You can add more if needed to ensure the colour and flavour is right.) Pop the rice to one side and take the cooked meat mixture off the heat. Taste it and add in a little salt and pepper if necessary.

5 Preheat the oven to 160°C/gas 3. Spoon half the rice into a casserole to get a nice layer at the bottom before spooning in half of the sauce, then another layer of rice and finally the remainder of the sauce. Cover the dish with a lid and pop into the oven to cook for a further 40 minutes, by which time the meat will be lovely and tender and the whole lot – rice, veg, sauce and beef – will have mixed and blended together to make an exceptionally tasty curry. Serve up with some chopped coriander on top for a final taste explosion.

BOILING VESSEL

Bully Beef and Boiled Sweets wouldn't be complete without something being written about our favourite national pastime. No, I'm not talking about queuing in the post office or moaning about the weather: we are, of course, referring to a good old-fashioned cuppa. Just as at home, a mug of tea is an instant pick-me-up for any soldier, and one of the most sought-after commissions in the Forces is to be placed in a vehicle with a 'boiling vessel'. Found in armoured tanks like the Challenger and Warrior, as well as smaller and nippier vehicles like the Land Rover, a boiling vessel is a water-heating system, wired directly to the vehicle's battery, that produces instant hot water. It might not sound like much, but such small luxuries can mean the world to a serving man or woman (especially when the alternative means using the more time-consuming and more fiddly stove/mess-tin method.)

So important is a boiling vessel it's even responsible for generating its own special, completely non-official, army rank – the 'BV Commander'. Given to a new recruit often venturing out on their first mission, it fair swells the heart and blushes the cheek of the recipient when bestowed with such a fancy-sounding title. Shoulders slump somewhat when they realise it just means keeping the rest of the crew provided with teas and coffees all day. (Thanks to www. arrse.co.uk for this information.) But its relevance doesn't just end with us Brits: our American allies in Iraq and Afghanistan have also fallen for this little bit of kit too. US captains noticed that we Brits were brewing up even in the middle of live-fire missions – always time for a brew, even in the middle of heavy shelling – and noticed how cool our guys were under these conditions. They soon ordered BVs be fitted to their own armoured vehicles.

If this idea has whetted your appetite you can buy ex-army models quite easily on the web, and they will only set you back about £30. Not sure how well they'll wire into a Vauxhall Corsa, though . . .

LASAGNE

Is it just us, or do you suspect that those posh waiters in those frighteningly expensive Italian restaurants aren't actually, well, 'Italian'? You know the sort: trousers so tight they're doing irreparable harm to their swingers, who wax lyrical about the breathtaking architecture of Milan and who turn on the thickest, roguish Italian accent when taking food orders from anyone female who's blessed with a pulse. It is our considered opinion, though, that this is all a ruse. That, in fact, their real names are Barry and Trevor, that the most authentically Italian thing they've done is order a double pepperoni pizza from Domino's, and as soon as they are back in their restaurant's kitchen, the accent drops and they revert to thickest, broadest Brummie. These thoughts are particularly fitting because, just like those possible imposters, lasagne may not be, actually, Italian. There are a couple of theories on the alternative origins of this super-tasty meal. The

first has it that it originated in Italy's close European neighbour Greece and they stole it from them. Greece cooked a surprisingly similar dish, with strips of pasta dough between meat and cheese layers, and called it 'Laganon'. More than that, the Greeks called the pot they cooked Laganon in 'Lasana' – both words, we're sure you'll agree, aren't a million miles away from the word we use now. The second theory is even better because – break out the red, white and blue bunting – the dish may be, in fact, British! For right there in Britain's oldest known cookbook – *The Forme of Cury*, a 700-year-old scroll written during the reign of King Richard II from recipes created by the king's master chefs, there is a dish called 'Loseyn', which again follows a similar meat, cheese and dough stacking system.

Regardless of its birthplace, the dish is delicious and is beloved by the British Forces, hence its inclusion here. This version is made from Menu Box B.

For four servings

You will need:

For the tortillas (in place of pasta sheets):
225g plain flour
warm water

For the sauce:
good knob of butter
4 tablespoons plain flour
450ml milk (the Forces use reconstituted milk powder)
250g cheese, grated (the type of cheese is up to your particular taste buds. A good Cheddar is always good for lasagne and it's what the Army uses. A more Italian vibe would mean going for mozzarella for gooeyness, mixed with a couple of handfuls of grated Parmesan for extra cheesy bite)
salt and pepper

For the filling:

400g minced beef (the Forces use canned minced beef and onion)

1 onion (if using fresh mince)

2 garlic cloves, crushed (the Forces use ½ teaspoon garlic powder)

splash of olive oil

400g can of chopped tomatoes (the Forces use reconstituted tomato powder)

1 tablespoon tomato purée

good pinch of dried mixed herbs

How you do it:

1   Instead of pasta sheets separating the ingredients, the Army make their own tortillas instead (nothing if not resourceful, our lads and lasses). You can, of course, buy pre-made lasagne sheets if you so desire and use those, but for the more authentic army approach, you need to make tortillas from the flour and water. Pile the flour on a work surface, create a little well in the middle of it and slowly add warm water to it, mixing with your hands until it starts getting to the consistency of Play-Doh. Keep adding water if it's too stiff or flour if it's too runny. When you are happy with the consistency, roll it out into thin-ish sheets approx. the same size as the dish you will be cooking the lasagne in, and cook each tortilla quickly on both sides in a hot, dry frying pan until they are dried out and speckled brown. Once they are done put to one side.

2   Now make a white cheesy sauce. Melt the butter in a saucepan. Stir in the flour and keep on cooking for a minute or two. Take the pan off the heat and gradually stir in the milk so there are no lumps, then pop it back on the heat and cook, stirring all the time until it's thickened and bubbling. Stir in 150g of the cheese and some salt and pepper and put it to one side.

3   Next, in a separate saucepan, fry the minced beef (if using fresh mince) with the onion and garlic in a splash of olive oil for 10 minutes or so, stirring to ensure it is browned all the way through and crumbly, not lumpy. The Army use canned minced beef and onion, which just needs heating up and so is quicker and works just as well – the choice is yours.

4   When the mince is ready, add the canned tomatoes (or rehydrated tomato powder), tomato purée and, finally, some mixed herbs and stir it all together. Let it blip away for 15 minutes.

5   Now comes the fun 'Bob the Builder' bit – the layering up. First, preheat the oven to 180°C/gas 4. Start with a thin layer of meaty sauce in your chosen ovenproof dish, then add a thin layer of cheese sauce and top off with a tortilla sheet. Then start another layer of meat, cheese and tortilla and keep going until you reach the top of your dish. You should finish off with a layer of cheese sauce. Lastly, smother the top with the remaining grated cheese.

6   Pop the lasagne into the oven for 35–40 minutes or until the top cheesy layer is all golden and brown, and serve immediately.

THE HORROR BAG

It's not just schoolchildren and forty-year-old men who still live with their parents who are sent out into the world with a packed lunch nestled about their person. Our very own army boys and girls are also regularly festooned with one when going on manoeuvres – the afore-mentioned 'Horror Bag'. The excellently entertaining, often hilarious, accidentally informative and, in places, very NSFW Army Rumour Service website (www.arrse.co.uk) has much to say about these little beauties. The UK's biggest online army community tells us civvies that while these 'Horror Bags' may look innocent enough – taking the form of the sort of white cardboard box you get a delicatessen's fine cheese or delicate pastry in – the truth is somewhat different. For, rather than being filled to the brim with mouth-watering goodies, the Horror Bag's name is well earned.

You would imagine that, on the grounds that soldiers are tough as nails and also have to run around a fair bit, any lunch they are given to eat while out on operations would be something hearty, warm and filling (to replace those lost calories) and, perhaps, also bring a sense of comfort in such potentially depressing circumstances. Sadly not the Horror Bag. Listed below is what you could find yourself face to face with. (It's worth pointing out, this list is an amalgamation of all the things that possibly come in HBs, so you wouldn't be confronted with all this in one go. Most soldiers would thank their lucky stars that's the case. We couldn't possibly comment . . .)

Two sandwiches Cheese is a preferred ingredient, as is egg mayonnaise, but nine times out of ten, one sarnie will contain the special army ingredient known by the troops as 'Mystery Fish': a fishy paste whose piscine origins are hard to put your finger on. It's certainly not a species that has featured in nearly sixty years of David Attenborough documentaries.

One packet of crisps Flavours range from salt and vinegar all the way to cheese and onion (no 'sweet chilli chicken' or 'balsamic vinegar and cracked black pepper' here). Also no Walkers or Kettle Chips – it is always, sadly, an unknown brand.

An apple If it didn't start covered in bruises, by the time it's rattled around in a Bergen backpack for a few hours, it will have them by lunchtime.

A can of soft drink Again, the Coca-Colas and Pepsis of the world are eschewed in favour of the British-made Panda Cola. We're quite sure this is a decision based on national pride and not cost-cutting (ahem).

A pot of yoghurt Many a man has longed for yoghurt when he is cold and tired and in need of sustenance. Oh no, that's right, our mistake, that's never happened. But that's all right, because your average yoghurt pot is practically indestructible and will easily survive hours of living in a backpack while the wearer yomps across the unforgiving landscape. Oh no, our mistake again, it's just thin plastic and a sliver of foil – all of which leads to the inevitable yoghurt-coated bag contents.

One pasty Research suggests that, once upon a time, these were Ginster pies, but they now tend to be non-branded variations that appear not to have been within miles of a Cornish postcode. Geographical variations exist – northern divisions will sometimes have a sausage roll instead. Either option is likely to be just the wrong side of frozen.

One chocolate biscuit The one concession to a recognised name, this will be a Kit Kat, Blue Riband, Penguin or Wagon Wheel biscuit and complete pot luck as to which you receive.

Once the Horror Bags are distributed, there then begins the age-old ritual of swapping items with colleagues to get a combination of the above that is to your liking.

66 … the Horror Bag's name is well earned. **99**

BEEF FAJITAS

The beauty of the fajita (outside of the simple food arithmetic of cheese + meat + spice = awesomeness) is its portability. Like a much more delicious piece of fruit or a pimped-up sandwich, the fajita – once rolled – can be held in one hand and taken with you wherever you go (particularly useful when you are in a combat zone and you may need to haul ass at a moment's notice). Presumably that, plus the fact it's easy to cook, is the reason for its regular appearance on Forces' menus around the world. Here is a recipe made using the ingredients in Menu Box C.

For four servings

You will need:
500g beef steak (the Forces use canned minced beef and onion, which you can use instead. If you are not a fan of beef, then chicken breast, cut into strips and quickly stir-fried, works just as well)
a little olive oil
1 teaspoon chilli powder if you like it hot, or less if you like it milder (you can, of course, use a fresh chilli, deseeded and chopped instead)
2 garlic cloves, finely chopped (the Forces use ½ teaspoon garlic powder)

1 teaspoon dried mixed herbs
splash of Tabasco
salt and pepper
1 large onion (the Forces use rehydrated dried onion) – remember to put some aside for the salsa
1 red pepper

For the tortillas:
225g plain flour
warm water

For the salsa:
400g can of chopped tomatoes
chopped fresh coriander (this isn't in the Forces recipe so is a tasty but optional extra)
squeeze of lime juice (optional)

To finish:
shredded lettuce (the Forces don't always have access to this, so this is an optional extra)
grated cheese

> " The fajita . . . simple food arithmetic of cheese + meat + spice = awesomeness. "

How you do it:

1 The Forces use canned minced beef and onion, which will make for an excellent and quick alternative to steak. But if you can afford it, and you want to have bigger chunks of meat in your fajita, then grab yourself a steak. You don't have to break the bank as fajitas work well with the cheaper, frying steaks, as you are cutting them into thin strips when cooking. Whichever meat option you choose, pop it into a shallow bowl. For the steak, rub it over a little olive oil, before adding in the chilli powder (not too much if you aren't a fan of a high heat), the garlic powder (or chopped garlic), the mixed herbs (ideally a bit of chopped coriander too but the Forces don't always get their hands on this, so don't worry if you can't), a splash of Tabasco (to taste – again be careful if you don't want it too spicy) and some salt and pepper. Make sure the meat is well mixed and coated with the marinade and then set to one side for it all to soak in and get really tasty while you crack on with the veg. (For canned mince, simply

mix in the other flavouring ingredients, omitting the olive oil.)

2 Pre-heat the grill or a griddle pan on a moderate heat, and then cut the onion and red pepper into man-sized chunks (keep a few pieces of onion to finely chop for the salsa). If you are

using the grill, just pop them under for 10 minutes or so until the red pepper's skin is starting to char and the onion is going golden brown, turning once or twice. If you are going the griddle pan way, toss the chopped veg in a little olive oil before putting them in the

hot pan, again for about 10 minutes. (Always oil the food, not the griddle pan, that way you don't get a smoke-filled kitchen.)

3 When the veg is ready, remove from the grill or griddle but leave whichever pan you are using on the heat, as you will be returning to grill the meat soon. When the peppers have cooled, carefully peel the charred bits off and then pop both them and the onion on a plate covered in foil to keep them warm until ready to eat.

4 Now for the tortillas. You can, of course, use ready-made but it's very easy to make your own as the Forces do. First things first, you make a dough from the flour and water. Pile the flour on a work surface, create a little well in the middle of it and slowly add warm water to it, mixing with your hands until it starts getting to the consistency of Play-Doh. Keep adding water if it's too stiff or flour if it's too runny. When you are happy with the consistency, divide the dough into balls and roll

them out to about 20cm discs, roughly the same size as a small dinner plate, and cook each tortilla quickly on both sides in a dry pan until they are just cooked and faintly speckled brown but not too crisp. Wrap them in foil to soften them and keep them warm until ready to roll.

5 Now to the meat. If you are using steak, fish it out of the marinade and grill for just 2–3 minutes on each side for a medium finish. Add a little longer for well-done and a little less for rare. Leave the steak to rest for a couple of minutes on a plate covered in foil (to keep in some of the heat and allow it to get really juicy and tenderised). If you are using the marinated canned mince, put it into a small pan and heat through over a low heat for a few minutes until piping hot before serving.

6 The final ingredient you need to make before you start rolling fajitas is the salsa. Once more, you can buy ready-made but the Forces make their own and so will we. Empty the can

of chopped tomatoes into a bowl. (If you like your salsa smooth, then chop through the tomatoes again or blitz in a blender. You can, of course, use 4 fresh tomatoes if you prefer.) Next, pop in the bit of reserved chopped onion and mix together. Add a pinch of salt and pepper and a hit of chilli powder – again to your taste and level of preferred heat. If you have any coriander, add this in now (another non-Forces ingredient would be a squeeze of fresh lime juice for added zing) and mix the lot together.

7 Now the fun part – making the fajitas. Slice the steak into thin strips. Take a tortilla, add in a few of the steak strips or a spoonful of the hot, spiced minced beef, a little of the char-grilled onion and pepper, a spoonful of the salsa, a sprinkling of chopped lettuce and finish off with grated cheese. Roll the lot up the best you can and shove it into your, by now, salivating mouth. Repeat filling, rolling and munching until stuffed.

PINEAPPLE CRUMBLE AND CUSTARD

As the teeth-grindingly, sphincter-tighteningly, fist-squeezingly annoying TV meerkat would have it, this recipe is most definitely 'simples'. Due to its simplicity, this dessert is very popular across army bases, with the added bonus that it is also quick to prepare. Both factors which make it a great beginner's dish for those novice cooks among you as it involves very few ingredients and not a huge amount of preparation beyond mixing stuff together in a bowl. However, don't let that fool you into thinking it won't taste very nice – this is a little cracker and it's all made from the ingredients in Box E.

For four servings

You will need:
500g can of pineapple slices
250g strawberry fruit bars
200g margarine, softened
200g porridge oats
300g caster sugar
1 packet of instant custard

How you do it:
1 Preheat the oven to 220°C/gas 7. Drain the can of pineapple, reserving the juice as you'll need some of it in a short while. Put the pineapple into a baking dish and crumble in the strawberry fruit bars, ensuring the two are well mixed together. Next, pour in a little of the reserved juice to keep it all moist.
2 Put the margarine and the porridge oats in a bowl and rub together with your fingers (like when making pastry). After the oats are all worked in, add the sugar and give it one final mix. (It's easier to do all this in a food processor if you have one, but if you don't then be prepared for the fact your mitts will get good and sticky.)
3 Cover the pineapple and fruit bar mixture with a thick layer of the crumbly oats and bake the whole lot for 40–45 minutes or until the crumble is golden brown on top. Serve with the instant custard (just follow the packet's instructions) for an easy but top-drawer tasting result. All this and not an irritating insurance-hawking mammal in sight . . .

CHILLI CON CARNE

There are few more manly dishes than chilli con carne. Good, stodgy fare that can warm the soul and fill the belly of even the largest of men, and so it's no surprise that this is a favourite of the Forces' chefs. So good is it for men and women preparing to do battle that the dish has long been linked with soldiers and armies. As early as the 1500s there is record of one Native American tribe who were so confident of victory in a forthcoming battle against the invading conquistadors that they had already prepared cauldrons of tomatoes, salt and chillies in anticipation of a victory feast. As the eagle-eyed among you will note, though, there is a key missing ingredient – meat. However, our Native American brothers had thought of that. The meat was to be supplied by the conquistadors themselves – out of their own flesh. Here, then, is a recipe using the ingredients in Menu Box C to make a dish that can satisfy even the biggest appetite, and with the added bonus of not having to resort to cannibalism.

For four servings

You will need:
1 large onion (the Forces use rehydrated dried onion)
1 red pepper
a little vegetable or sunflower oil
400g minced beef (the Forces use canned minced beef and onion)
340g can of Spam, chopped
2 garlic cloves (the Forces use ½ teaspoon garlic powder)
dried mixed herbs
1 teaspoon chilli powder if you like it hot, or less if you like it mild. (You can, of course, instead use a fresh chilli, deseeded and chopped)
400g can of chopped tomatoes
400g can of red kidney beans, drained
salt and pepper
500g long-grain rice

How you do it:
1 Chop the onion into whatever sized chunks or slices you prefer – we think a chilli is one dish that can handle

> **"** Good, stodgy fare that can warm the soul and fill the belly of even the largest of men … **"**

really man-size bits of onion but the choice is yours. The Forces version uses rehydrated pre-chopped onion. If you want to go that route, just soak the onion in warm water for the length of time the packet suggests. Next, cut off the top from the red pepper – stalk and all – and discard it, then cut the pepper in half lengthways, remove the seeds and white pith, which can be quite bitter if left in. Once that's done, chop it up and pop the veg to one side.

2   Now on to the meat. Start by putting a pan on a medium heat and add a splash of oil. If you are using fresh beef mince, then brown it with the onion and red pepper for 7–8 minutes or so to ensure all the mince is cooked and there are no pink bits left. Just keep stirring and breaking the mince up into smaller pieces with a wooden spoon until you are happy it is all cooked through and crumbly, not lumpy. If you are using canned minced beef (which usually comes in a gravy) as the Forces do, then just fry off the onion and pepper until the onion is soft and translucent,

then add the canned mince and heat through, stirring.

3   At this point you have a choice whether to double the meat ration or keep it as it is. The Forces, of course, prefer their meals to be hearty and filling, and so, here they also add the chopped Spam to the dish. It's is up to you. Now stir in the garlic, a sprinkling of mixed herbs and the amount of chilli powder to suit your desire for heat. Give it a good stir and leave to bubble and blip for 5 minutes or so.

4   Next, add the can of chopped tomatoes – juice and all – followed by the kidney beans and a good pinch of salt and pepper. Stir it all again, pop a lid on the pan and let it simmer for 20 minutes to really allow the flavours to develop. Keep an eye on it, though, during this time – you don't want it to dry out, burn or stick to the pan bottom. If it looks like it's getting too dry just add a splash of water and keep stirring – the sauce should

look thick and juicy when it's done. While you are simmering the chilli, get some water on the boil, chuck in a pinch of salt and cook the rice for 10 minutes or according to packet directions, then drain in a colander and sit it back on the saucepan to keep hot.

5   When the chilli is cooked and you are happy with the sauce consistency (go a little longer if you need) taste and add a little more salt, pepper or even chilli powder to get it flavoured right. Once you have it where you want it, serve a generous dollop in the middle of a bed of rice and get stuck in.

FISH BALLS

There are many strange facts, trivia and phenomena associated with the British military. Consider this little morsel: the lance only ceased to be an official battle weapon of the British Army in 1927. Also, the shortest war in history was that between Britain and Zanzibar in 1896, which was all over in 38 minutes when Zanzibar's only warship, the ageing *Glasgow*, was sunk by two well-aimed shells. Or that during WWII the very first bomb the British dropped on Germany killed the only elephant in Berlin Zoo. But nothing is so strange as to find out that, not only do fish have balls, the British Forces delight in serving them to our troops in a curry sauce. This is made using the ingredients in Menu Box A.

For four servings

You will need:
125g plain flour, plus extra for dusting
½ teaspoon salt
150ml water
pepper (preferably freshly ground)
1 large potato (or instant mashed potato for authenticity)
400g long-grain rice
splash of olive oil
1 large onion, chopped (the Forces use rehydrated dried onion)
185g can of tuna, drained
300g can of garden peas, drained
2 garlic cloves, crushed (the Forces use ½ teaspoon garlic powder)
1 teaspoon curry powder (or 1 packet of curry-flavoured instant noodles)
1 litre vegetable or sunflower oil for deep-frying

How you do it:

1 As with all good fried food you need to start by making a great batter. Batter can be pimped with all manner of stuff – ice-cold lager, mustard powder, white wine, paprika – but this is a simple version, which takes the fewest ingredients and the shortest amount of faffing about. Once you have mastered this you can add in any of the afore-mentioned ingredients and use it to batter fish, vegetables, or, if you are from Scotland, anything you like.

2 Start by mixing the flour (you will need to leave a little to dust the surface you are going to be working on later) with the salt in a big bowl. Once mixed, make a well in the centre of the salty flour and slowly add the water, whisking it constantly to make a thick, smooth batter with no lumps. (You can always add a drop or two more water if it's still lumpy. And if you go too far the other way and the batter becomes too watery, add a little more flour.) Once you are happy with the consistency – dip a spoon into it and the batter should coat and stick to it, and not all run off – crack in a little black pepper for added flavour. Pop it to one side for now while you make the fish balls.

3 Put two pans of salted water on the go. One for our mashed potato (peel, chop, boil and mash if you are using a fresh spud; follow the packet directions if you are using dried potato as the Forces do) and one for the rice (cook per the packet's instructions, then drain in a colander, cover with a lid and keep warm over the pan). While that's happening – and who said men can't multi-task? – heat the olive oil over a medium heat in a pan. To that add the chopped onion, or the rehydrated dried onion (dry it first on kitchen paper), and fry until golden brown. Remove from the heat and add the drained tuna and peas. Next in the assembly line, add the mashed potato, garlic and the curry powder. (Add a little more or a little less depending on how hot you like it.) The Forces – because they are ingenious – use the sachet of flavouring that is supplied with a packet of instant noodles

instead of curry powder. Feel free to do the same and save the noodles for another day. Mix the lot well and season with a little salt and pepper.

4 Let the mixture cool a little, then tip it out onto a work surface that has been lightly dusted with flour (to stop the balls from sticking) and start rolling the lot up into little ball shapes – aim for them to be just a little bigger than a golf ball so they won't take very long to fry.

5 If you have a deep-fat fryer, follow its instructions for perfectly crispy balls, but if you don't have one, fear not – there's an easy way to do it without buying all new kit. Take a big saucepan – one with high sides to prevent any hot oil splashing out – and empty in the 1 litre of vegetable or sunflower oil. (At this point, we are going to assume you are a semi-sensible adult and aren't going to be throwing hot oil about or ducking your head into the pot any time soon. Short version: hot oil = dangerous.) Okay, whack up the heat and get the oil going. A good way to know when it's hot enough to fry is to drop a piece

of the peeled potato skin, if you haven't thrown it away, or a cube of bread into it. If it floats, sizzles and browns in 30 seconds, then the oil is ready to go. Dip each ball in the batter, making sure they all get a good coating. Carefully lower them into the oil and let them deep-fry for a few minutes, gently moving them around, until they are golden brown all over. Slowly fish them out with a slotted spoon, drain on kitchen paper and serve on a bed of the boiled rice.

THE TWENTY-FOUR-HOUR RATION PACK

We know plenty of blokes who, presented with their entire food consumption for twenty-four hours in one handy-to-carry package, would find themselves face to face with the depressing sight of four packets of crisps, a slice of toast, some Haribo and a doner kebab. (And that's just on a Monday: imagine the horrors of collecting together Saturday's intake!) In the Forces, though, this actually happens. When a soldier is set to be away from his or her barracks/base/post for a considerable period of time, they are issued with twenty-four-hour ration packs to see them through. These are staples of the British Army and have been giving soldiers everything they need – and some stuff they didn't – for over a century. Back in 2008 the ration pack had a Gok Wan-style makeover designed to combat 'menu fatigue' (the squaddies were bored to tears with the food). Out went some very long-standing but generally unpopular choices like 'biscuits brown' (designed originally as a bread substitute, the crackers were so tough that they were ideal as an emergency snack or for repairing bomb damage in army vehicles) and the more stodgy hot puddings such as treacle sponge (as lovely as they sound, not so good to eat in the middle of the punishing heat of an Iraqi desert) – and in came more modern dishes such as green Thai curry and beef teriyaki. Produced for the British Army by Vestey Foods (you can buy your very own from their website, http://rations.vesteyfoods.com for the princely sum of £15.36 per twenty-four-hour pack), the rations now come in twenty different varieties (thirty-eight if you also count the six Sikh/Hindu, six vegetarian and six halal options), which showcase quite a mind-boggling array of choices. The packs contain everything a soldier needs over a day: three main meals plus snacks and a heap of energy drinks. It will deliver 4,000 calories per man or woman (around twice as many as we are advised to take on board, but then we aren't running around with a full Bergen on our backs and getting shot at). The food can be eaten hot or cold and now comes in foil packs rather than the heavy and cumbersome tins of yore, so it can be stored in pockets and pouches rather than take up valuable space in the backpack.

With the aim of being completist, here's a mega-list of what you can find across all twenty basic ration packs. You'll see there is a helluva lot of variety and it all sounds very appetising indeed. Although, after researching, dissecting and listing all this lot, we feel we need to go for a little lie-down in a darkened room to recover.

THE LIST

All ration packs start with the following same, basic ingredients:

1 pack of 10 tissues
1 packet of boiled sweets
1 re-useable poly bag
2 coffee sachets
1 x 6-pack water-purification tablets
3 packets chewing gum (peppermint
    or spearmint flavour)
1 spoon
4 sachets of sugar
2 disinfectant wipes
4 sachets beverage whitener
1 box waterproof matches
2 teabags

The rest of the ingredients below are divided across the twenty packs and the number after them shows in how many ration packs they appear. So in alphabetical order:

All-day breakfast (2)
Apple and cinnamon bar (2)

Apple drink (7)
Apple and peach fruit purée (3)
Apple, raspberry and blackcurrant
    fruit purée (2)
Apricot fruit bar (3)
Apricot health bar (1)
Apricot jam (6)
Banana health bar (1)
Beef Bolognese and pasta shells (2)
Beef goulash (1)
Beef jerky teriyaki (4)
Beef stroganoff (1)
Blackcurrant-flavoured water (9)
Blueberry health bar (1)
Caramel energy bar (5)
Carrot and coriander soup (1)
Cherry isotonic drink (13)
Chicken massaman potato curry –
    a Thai curry that's heavy on the
    tamarind and coconut milk (1)
Chicken and mushroom pasta (1)
Chicken panang – another Thai
    curry (1)
Chicken sausage and beans (2)
Chicken sweet and sour (1)
Chicken tikka (1)
Chicken tomato pasta (1)

Chicken and vegetable soup (2)

Chilli con carne (1)

Chocolate pudding in chocolate sauce (1)

Chunky bean and bacon soup (4)

Cranberry energy bar (2)

Dark chocolate-chip biscuit (3)

Digestive biscuit (3)

Exotic isotonic drink – we wonder how 'exotic' they really are (16)

Fig health bar (1)

Fruit cake (2)

Fruit and nut mix (4)

Fruit cocktail in pineapple juice (2)

Fruit cocktail in syrup (5)

Fruit and oat snack bar (4)

Fruitful muesli (2)

Fruity oatie biscuit (3)

Ginger crunch biscuit (3)

Golden oat bar (5)

Hot chocolate – mint (5)

Hot chocolate – orange (4)

Hot chocolate – regular (10)

Just Fruit – nope, your guess is as good as ours (4)

Kiwi, passion fruit and apple fruit purée (5)

Lamb curry (1)

Lamb hotpot (1)

Leek and potato soup (2)

Lemon energy drink (1)

Lucozade – orange isotonic (8)

Mango, banana, apple fruit purée (6)

Mango cake (1)

Mexican tuna pasta (2)

Mixed nuts (4)

Mushroom omelette (1)

Natural muesli (2)

Nut-mix health bar (1)

Oatmeal block (4)

Oreos (6)

Paella (1)

Pasta bolognese (1)

Pasta salad (2)

Peach drink (1)

Pear health bar (1)

Pilau rice (2)

Pineapple in syrup (2)

Plum jam (4)

Pork curry Gurka-style (1)

Pork sausage and beans (2)

Potato and beans (1)

Raisin health bar (1)

Raspberry energy drink (6)

Raspberry-flavoured water (10)

Rice (7)

Rice pudding (2)

Sausage casserole (1)

Sliced peaches in syrup (2)

Sliced pears in Syrup (1)

Strawberry, banana and apple fruit purée (3)

Strawberry health bar (1)

Strawberry jam (8)

Steak and vegetables (1)

Tabasco, green (9)

Tabasco, red (10)

Thai green vegetable curry (1)

Toasted muesli (3)

Toffee pudding in toffee sauce (1)

Tomato and basil soup (2)

Tropical-flavoured drink (1)

Tropical fruit mix (4)

Tuna chilli pasta (2)

Tuna in light mayo (9)

Tuna with lime and pepper (3)

Tuna pasta and beans (2)

Vegetarian all-day breakfast (2)

Vegetarian tomato noodle (1)

Yellow chicken curry (1)

CHEESE, HAM AND ONION PASTY

Ah, the humble pasty: bringing well-earned sustenance to hard-working men and women in tough and inhospitable situations. Fittingly, they began life as the preferred foodstuff of Cornish miners who loved the fact they could a) be easily carried and eaten without cutlery – the thick crust on the edge allowed them a place to hold the pasty so as not to get any dirt on their grub; b) the dense-packed ingredients would keep warm for ages; and c) they could serve as a full main meal and a cheeky dessert with one savoury end and one sweet. No surprise, then, that, unlike other Cornish inventions such as scrumpy or scowling at tourists, this filling and hardy dish has been warmly embraced by the British Forces. This is made using the ingredients in Menu Box E.

For four servings

You will need:

For the pastry:
500g plain flour
salt and pepper
dried mixed herbs
250g margarine, cut in small
    pieces
cold water
1 egg, beaten (the Forces use
    powdered egg that has been
    reconstituted with a little water)

For the filling:
splash of olive oil
1 large onion, sliced (the Forces use
    rehydrated dried onion)
4 or 5 cup mushrooms, sliced
340g can of ham, cut in smallish
    cubes
1 garlic clove, crushed (the Forces
    use ¼ teaspoon garlic powder,
    or to taste)
grated cheese

How you do it:
1   All good pasties start with good pastry, so let's get cracking. Put the flour, a pinch of salt and 1 teaspoon of dried mixed herbs into a large bowl and add the margarine. Lightly massage it in with the flour using your fingertips and thumbs (you will get messy) until it looks like breadcrumbs. Next, add cold water a little bit at a time. You want just enough to bind the dough together, so stop when you get to that point. It needs to be roughly the consistency of plasticine, so if you need more water splash a bit more in until you are there. Finally, wrap the whole lot in clingfilm and chill in the fridge for 20 minutes – the pastry is much easier to work with when it is cold. Once chilled, roll the pastry out and cut it into 18–20cm discs and put them back in the fridge while you make the filling.
2   The Forces use pre-cooked ingredients that only take a bit of prepping (the dried onion, for example, needs soaking in water before cooking but no peeling and chopping involved)

> **"the humble pasty: bringing well-earned sustenance to hard-working men and women in tough and inhospitable situations ..."**

and so they would simply mix all the ingredients for the filling together before moving on to the making of the pasty itself. Nothing wrong with that at all and this dish will taste absolutely grand if you wish to go that route, but there is another way that involves a wee bit more cooking, and here's how to do it.

3 Heat a splash of olive oil in a frying pan and add the sliced onion and mushrooms. When they are starting to ever so slightly bronze, remove from the heat. Stir in the ham, garlic, a good pinch of dried mixed herbs, and the cheese. Season well with pepper. (You probably won't need any salt as the ham is quite salty, but you can always taste a little bit and add some if you need it.) Pop the pan to one side while you move on to the building of the pasty.

4 Preheat the oven to 200°C/gas 6 and take the pastry discs out of the fridge. Pop each one onto a surface that has been dusted with flour (to stop them sticking) and put a quarter of the filling into the centre of each – you need

to leave a gap around the edge of the pasty to ensure you can seal it. Brush a little beaten egg around the edge of the pastry before carefully folding the disc in half and then sealing the top to the bottom. There are many tricks you can employ here but the simplest is just to squeeze the pastry together with your fingers. If you so desire, you can make it look 'pretty' afterwards by pushing the prongs of a fork all the way around the joined edges to crimp them.

5 Place the pasties on a baking sheet. Paint each pasty over with a little more of the beaten egg (this will make them look golden and shiny when cooked) and place the tray in the centre of the oven for 10 minutes to get everything started. Then drop the temp down to 160°C/gas 3 and cook for a further 40 minutes until crisp and golden brown. Serve warm from the oven. Delicious.

THE GROWLER

As we have said before, there are many ways that a member of Her Majesty's Forces can find themselves being fed. One such option is the Growler, and it's not something we wager you'll find listed in any other cookbook, anywhere else in the world. Once more we have the Army Rumour Service to thank for letting us into this little military secret.

This culinary delight is part of the staple diet of many serving men and women and is a warm, soggy pie or pasty bought at one of the many vending machines scattered about base camp. The contents of said Growler are shrouded in mystery. All that is known is that it is some form of 'meat', but from which animal it originates is not clear. Equally unclear until it's taken hold of is the temperature of your Growler, varying as it does from practically frozen to rip-the-skin-off-the-roof-of-your-mouth hot. The Growler experience is said to be marginally improved by covering it in the sachet condiment of your choosing – red, brown, mayo or mustard – before scoffing down in as few mouthfuls as possible.

So there you have it, 'the Growler', a true one-off for *Bully Beef and Boiled Sweets*.

SPAM FRITTERS

There have been many famous incidences of extreme bravery shown by the British Army in life-threatening circumstances. There was the Battle of Rorke's Drift – made famous by the Michael Caine movie *Zulu* – where just over one hundred British soldiers successfully defended their garrison against an intense assault by five thousand Zulu warriors, and in doing so, earned more Victoria Crosses for one regiment in one battle than ever before.

There was Group Captain Sir Douglas Bader, who, as a Spitfire pilot in WWII, fought in the Battle of Britain, secured twenty-two aerial 'kills' and successfully escaped from a prisoner-of-war camp. What's more, he did all this despite the fact he had lost both his legs in a flying accident years before. (In typical stiff-upper-lip fashion he recorded the fateful day in his diary thus: 'Crashed slow-rolling near ground. Bad show.' They don't make them like that any

more.) Then there is Royal Marine Lance Corporal Matt Croucher, who threw himself onto an exploding grenade to save the lives of his patrol. Croucher was in Helmand Province in Afghanistan when he tripped a Taliban booby-trap. He used his backpack to absorb the force of the explosion as his comrades dived for cover. The blast blew his rucksack more than 10m away but, remarkably, he suffered only a bloody nose.

Well, we wish to add a new hero to that list, one who has been so far the dictionary definition of 'unsung' and one after our very own culinary heart. We give you Corporal Liam Francis – a man who fed an entire battalion of the Welsh Guard for six weeks on nothing but Spam. Yes, Spam. The chopped-pork-and-ham product celebrated in Monty Python's famous sketch. Corporal Francis's moment came after the Taliban shot down a supply helicopter, destroying his battalion's rations and meals for the next forty-two days. However, being a

> **"** . . . a man who fed an entire battalion of the Welsh Guard for six weeks on nothing but Spam. Yes, Spam. **"**

member of the British Forces, Corporal Francis didn't bat an eyelid and showed the resourcefulness which our troops are rightly famous for – he cracked open can after can of what was left and got cooking. He knocked out Spam carbonara, Spam stroganoff, Spam stir-fry and the one you are going to try below – Spam fritters. The man deserves nothing less than a statue erected of him in his hometown of Tidworth. A statue made of Spam.

For four servings

You will need:
125g plain flour
pinch of salt
1 large egg
125ml beer (Corporal Francis
    would have had to make do
    with water, though)
340g can of Spam
vegetable or sunflower oil

How you do it:
1   Mix the flour, salt and egg in a bowl. Add in the beer (and drink the rest – see, cooking *is* fun!) Give it a good stir and you should end up with a good, thick 'cream'. (This is a variation of the basic batter mix outlined on page 60 in the Fish Balls recipe.)
2   Next cut the Spam into slices. Heat enough oil so you have about 5mm sat in a deep frying pan or wok. You can use more oil if you want or a deep-fat fryer, but, whatever you use, be very careful, as hot oil is extremely dangerous.
3   When the oil is good and hot, coat the Spam slices in the batter by dipping them into the bowl and letting the excess drain off, then carefully place them in the oil. Turn them over a couple of times during the next 3–4 minutes until they are crisp on the outside and golden brown. Drain on kitchen paper. Serve straightaway but be careful not to burn the skin off the roof of your mouth.

AROUND THE WORLD IN 80 RATION PACKS

The British Army are not the only ones to utilise a system of combat rations designed to be carried by troops into battle. Pretty much every standing army in the world has a version of the twenty-four-hour pack – something that is lightweight, easy to carry, contains a shedload of calories and takes minimal preparation before scoffing down. What is interesting are the international differences between each country's offerings. You know what's in our version, so here's a flavour of what to expect for dinner should you ever find yourself fighting for the Canadian, Finnish or Japanese Armies . . .

Canada They supply their boys and girls with the IMP (individual meal pack). As you go through these, you will see the military of the world show very little imagination when it comes to naming their packs.

They are, universally, 'does what it says on the tin' kinds of people. What's worth noting about the IMP is that, like the US version, it contains very generous portions and some cracking dishes – typical meals include a smoked-salmon fillet, scalloped potatoes and ham hock, and, even, a shepherd's pie.

Mexico The Mexican Army has the '*comida de combate individual diaria para soldados*' or 'individual soldier's daily combat meal box' (see what we mean about lack of imagination?). It uses an unusual system that only they, the Japanese and Malaysian armies employ, where you get one can of meat (beef, pork, chicken or fish in a sauce), which you then combine with the second tin, which houses the likes of rice, noodles, beans or pasta. They are also the only army to supply their troops with real cans of Coca-Cola. This is meant to be one of the best-tasting packs in any military, and when it was distributed by the Mexican Army to survivors of Hurricane Katrina, many Americans said it was some of the best food they'd ever had!

Colombia The *ración de campaña* (field rations) contains some awesome-sounding dishes, including *tamales* (leaf-wrapped cheese and meat pasties), *lentejas con chorizo* (chorizo with lentils) and *arroz atollado* (literally 'messy rice' – a pork or chicken risotto-type dish).

Finland The not-exactly-inspiring-sounding 'sissi rations' (*sissi* is Finnish for 'infantryman') doesn't contain very much, but then the Army is entirely conscripted and so meals can be counted upon to be served at base. If you do have to survive on the sissi ration, then be prepared for foil-packed crispbread, a small can of beef and some strong coffee. Best to fill up before you go out, then.

France As one would expect from such a culinary-renowned country, their RCIR (translated as 'reheatable individual combat rations') are the only ones in the world to come with a selection of hors d'oeuvres. You can expect salmon terrine, chicken-liver pâté and duck mousse. The main meals aren't bad, either, seeing the likes of veal Marengo (a veal stew) and *navarin d'agneau* (a great lamb and potato dish). Clearly people are signing up to the Foreign Legion not to forget a woman but to get their hands on the food.

Germany The *einmannpackung* (combat ration) does nothing to disavow national stereotypes, containing, as it does, at least four different sausage dishes. (For the record, these are: lentils with sausage, goulash with sausage, liver-sausage pâté and a dried meat sausage.)

Italy The *razione viveri speciali da combattimento* (special combat food ration) is another that sounds delicious as it serves its soldiers the likes of *tortellini al ragu, pasta a fagioli* and *insalata di riso*: all dishes that wouldn't be out of place on the menus of top notch restaurants.

Sweden The home of Ikea, not surprisingly, utilises some very minimalist methods to feed its soldiers. The *stridsportion* (field ration) uses a specially designed system by a company called DryTech that consists of freeze-dried meals labelled simply 'breakfast', 'lunch' and, you guessed it, 'dinner'.

Russia The IRP (individual ration packs) are unique in that they are the only ones in the world designed to simply keep a soldier alive. They contain enough calories to get by but the Army strictly forbids eating them for more than six days straight as the soldier would die from malnutrition. Considering it contains the likes of pea porridge concentrate, perhaps you'd end up starving not due to lack of vitamins but just out of choice.

Portugal The *ração individual de combate* (individual combat ration) is another good one to aim for as its army relies on maximum use of off-the-shelf supermarket items, many with the original label still on. Also a good one for fans of quince cream as it's the only one to contain it.

Israel Considering the volatile situation that its soldiers often find themselves in, it is not surprising that their Army supplies its troops with not only a 'Battle Ration', but

also an 'Ambush Ration' which contains little more than sweets and high-energy bars.

Australia The CR1M (combat ration 1 man) covers all the main Aussie food groups: a can of Foster's and a rugby ball. Only joking – it's another good one that contains the likes of Beef Kai Si Ming (an excellent curried mince dish) and an Anzac bar (a chewy coconut confection).

Japan We can't read Japanese but we presume the name is equally prosaic as the examples that have gone before. What we do know is what's in it and it is suitably rice-heavy. As with the Mexican example detailed before, you get two pouches, one containing some form of rice (plain, with mushrooms, or with veg) and a main-meal pouch with the likes of Yakitori chicken, mackerel in ginger sauce, or takana (mustard leaf) pickles and bamboo shoots.

China If there is one to definitely steer clear of it's the offering from the Chinese People's Liberation Army. Where all other ration packs come in at approximately 4,000 calories per soldier, the Chinese version is a paltry 1,000. An amount that, were you to eat in normal civvy life, would see you rapidly lose weight, as it is half the daily recommended intake for an adult. Worse than that, there isn't a prawn cracker in sight.

> **"** If there is one to definitely steer clear of it's the offering from the Chinese People's Liberation Army. **"**

CHOCOLATE GATEAU

The British Forces are many things – brave, tough, disciplined – but they are also great believers in the phrase 'necessity is the mother of invention'. Inhospitable locations and difficult circumstances have led to some great on-the-spot military innovations. Elsewhere in this book you'll read how pies have taken the place of heavy explosives and biscuits have been used to stop a case of the trots. Well, that 'can do' attitude also saw the birth of this sweet treat, for while the battlefields of Afghanistan remain a fair distance from the nearest Tesco, and basic rations don't include fancy cakes such as this, the Forces do what they always do – they invent their own. It's not a recipe that you would find in any other cookbook, as it's not a traditional way of making a gateau, but with the ingredients they have to hand this is a cracking eat. It won't win any prizes for its looks but it will taste great – and that's the most important thing. This is made using the contents of Menu Boxes A and D

For 6–8 servings

You will need:
310g canned chocolate sponge pudding
1 jar of strawberry jam
2 handfuls of mixed dried fruit
400g can of custard (or a packet of instant custard)
250g can of drinking chocolate powder
1 small chocolate bar of your choosing

How you do it:

1 Open the sponge tin top and bottom and gently push the cake out of the tin. If it doesn't want to budge, loosen it with a round-bladed knife. Don't worry if it comes out looking a little rough around the edges as it is just our starting block. Tip the sponge cake on its side and then carefully cut it into three roughly equal-sized layers. (Again, don't stress if it's not exact – you're not going to be entering this into any competitions: it's just for your eating pleasure.)

2 Next, spread strawberry jam all over the top and sides of each of the three layers. The only side you're not going to cover in jam is the bottom of each layer, and that's just because it would make a right old mess and stick to any plate or surface while you're working on it. Arrange each of the three layers next to one another on a clean work surface and, for an added bit of flavour, sprinkle two of the slices with the dried fruit mix.

> **❝** It won't win any prizes for its looks but it will taste great – and that's the most important thing. **❞**

3   Once that's done, re-stack the sponge cake on a plate, topping with the non-fruity slice, and pop it to one side. At this point in fancy dan recipes you would be asked to make up some kind of chocolate cream to spread all over the outside of the cake. Well, in the innovative spirit mentioned in the intro to this recipe, the British Forces do just that by making their own with custard and hot-chocolate powder. If it's powdered custard you are working with you'll need to make it up according to the packet directions; if it's the ready-made variety, you can, obviously, get straight to mixing in all the drinking chocolate. This will both turn the custard nice and chocolatey and will thicken it up too, which is a good thing as you are about to cover the whole cake in it.

4   Start by dumping big dollops on the top and then spread it over the surface with a round-bladed knife or the back of a spoon. Repeat for the sides but be prepared for a fair bit to slide off, just keep going until most is covered. Again, it's not something that looks pretty – just tastes damn good. When all the sides are covered, as a final flourish, grate the chocolate bar over the top of the cake and then get slicing and eating.

SEXY HEXY

Back at base (or for those lucky chaps stationed in a vehicle with a boiling vessel – see page 49), very little thought and time is given to how their meals and brews are going to be prepared. However, once out on patrol the troops' very livelihoods rely on a little something called hexamethylenetetramine, or 'hexy' for short. Hexy is a solid-fuel tablet that, once lit, sits on a fold-out metal stove and burns just long enough to knock up a cuppa or a spot of dinner. The hexamine stove was invented in Germany back in 1936 and has been used by the British Forces for donkey's years as it simply and effectively does the job. However, that is not to say that is doesn't have its downsides. Hexamine is made by combining two, non-human-friendly chemicals that go by the names of formaldehyde and ammonia. When you light the tablet, it therefore gives off gases from both these beauties plus an added bonus stench of hydrogen cyanide, which, when all combined, is enough to cause vomiting and, if it gets into your food, kidney damage. The heat given off from the tablets is also non-adjustable – so no chance of any sautéing or flambéing – and the stoves themselves are exceptionally sensitive to wind and damp. They also tend to coat whatever pot you are cooking in with a sticky dark goo. (However, we have it on good authority that a used tea bag rubbed on the cooled-down mess gets it off in a flash.) The question then remains, why does the British Army persevere with them? Well, put simply, they are cheap (you can buy one on the internet – eight hexy tablets and the fold-out metal stove –for as a little as a couple of quid); they are easy to use; lightweight to carry; and, also, provide an evening's entertainment in the form of 'Hexy Telly' (a trance-like state every soldier finds themselves in when staring into the flames of the stove on a long night's exercise).

GURKHAS' CHICKEN PILAU

The famously hard-as-nails Gurkhas have been a part of the British Armed Forces for almost 200 years. We first came across these exceptionally brave soldiers in our empire-building days, when they effectively held off an invading British Army for two years – eventually fighting us to a stalemate. It was the military equivalent of Great Wakering Rovers of the Ryman Isthmian Football League (Division One North) holding Manchester United to a draw in the FA Cup, every week, for two years. We Brits were so impressed by the Gurkhas – one British soldier at the time wrote: 'I never saw more bravery exhibited in my life. Run they would not and of death they seemed to have no fear, though their comrades were falling thick around them'– that we immediately made Nepal our protectorate and they've been fighting alongside us ever since. In WWII, more than 200,000 Gurkhas were on the Allies' side putting the willies right up the Germans with their covert tactics. Their favourite ploy was to break into Nazi barracks at night, and quietly slit the throat of the first soldier in the line of beds. They would then spare the next soldier but cut his bootlaces, before slitting the throat of the next and so on and so on all the way down the line. The first the Germans would know about the intrusion was when the 'lucky' soldiers woke up to find the men either side of them dead. They'd immediately panic and go for their boots, only to find the laces chopped – showing that they, too, could have been killed. Not surprisingly, quite a few didn't fancy going back to the Front after that. No such tactics are reported from their time spent fighting in Afghanistan (where our very own Prince Harry served with them during his ten weeks on the ground), but their toughness is still unquestioned – they have after all won twenty-six Victoria Crosses, not bad for a country with a population smaller than Morocco or Tanzania.

The Gurkhas are also famous for their traditional weapon, a 45cm-long curved knife known as the *kukri* that each soldier carries. It used to be the case that, once drawn from its scabbard, the knife had to 'taste blood' before being replaced, even if it meant the soldier slicing his own hand before holstering it. These days, and most apt for us, this no longer holds true and the knife is mainly used for cooking. While we don't suggest you prepare this traditional Gurkha dish while wielding a *kukri*, we imagine it is far more fun if you do. This recipe is slightly different from the others in this chapter as it isn't tied to a set menu box and so it includes a number of new ingredients and is a bit of a longer process. That being said, it's not scarily hard to do and we'll take you through it step by step until you end up with a corker of a dish.

For four servings

You will need:

2 large onions
½ teaspoon grated fresh ginger
2 garlic cloves, chopped
1 teaspoon poppy seeds (or black mustard seeds)
4 cloves

4 cardamon pods, split (green or
  black are fine)
150ml plain yoghurt
1 teaspoon ground coriander
salt and pepper
350g skinless chicken breasts,
  cut in cubes or strips
25g butter
400g long-grain rice
150ml milk
pinch of ground turmeric
chopped fresh coriander to garnish

> ❝ While we don't suggest you prepare this traditional Gurkha dish while wielding a *kukri*, we imagine it is far more fun if you do. ❞

How you do it:

1 Start by making your own curry paste, which we'll use to marinate the chicken. Chop up one of the onions and place it in a bowl with the grated ginger (you can buy this in a jar, or you can get the ginger fresh and peel and grate it yourself), the garlic, poppy or black mustard seeds, two of the cloves and two of the cardamom pods, the yoghurt and the ground coriander and a little salt and pepper.

2 Now use it to marinate the chicken – by which we mean give it a damn good rubbing all over with the paste – simply pop the chicken breasts in the mixture and start massaging. (Doing this helps the flavours from the paste to infuse the chicken and it also helps tenderise the meat itself.) Once they are suitably pummelled, leave the chicken to sit in the paste and let the whole lot marinate for an hour in the fridge.

3 When the time is nearly up, chop the other onion. Melt the butter in a frying pan on medium heat and when it's bubbling away, toss in the onion and fry until golden brown. Next, lift the pieces of chicken out of the marinade, add to the onion and fry, stirring, for 5 minutes until cooked through. When that's done, turn the heat right down and add in the remainder of the marinade and simmer the lot gently for 10–15 minutes. At this point add more salt or pepper until it tastes how you would like. While the curry is bubbling away, cook the rice in some boiling salted water that you have also added the remaining cardamom pods and cloves (they will help to flavour the rice).

4 Preheat the oven to 200°C/gas 6. When the rice is done, transfer the chicken and sauce into an ovenproof dish, cover it with the rice (removing the cloves and cardamom if you like). Mix the milk with the turmeric and pour over. Give it a mix through, cover with foil and pop the whole lot into the hot oven and cook for another 10 minutes before serving immediately with some chopped coriander sprinkled over to a table of salivating mates.

ITALIAN TUNA PIE

There are many misnomers in the modern Army. 'Friendly fire' isn't especially affable: it's hard to see how several hundred tonnes of bomber can be described as being 'stealth'. And don't get us started on why the Swiss Army need such a fabulous penknife. Well, the same goes for this fine dish. It may be entitled 'Italian Tuna Pie' but one suspects the closest it's been to the land of fine wines and pasta is a Pizza Express just outside of Birmingham. That's not to say, however, that it's not super-tasty, nor that it doesn't have a sprinkling of Italiano about it with its oregano and other such Italian herbs – just don't expect it to be popping up on Silvio Berlusconi's dinner plate any time soon. It is a simple but appetising recipe made using the ingredients in Menu Box A.

For four servings

You will need:

1 large onion, chopped (the Forces use rehydrated dried onion)
splash of olive oil
2 carrots
250g peas (fresh, frozen or drained, canned)
400g can of cream of tomato soup
small handful of fresh chopped basil or ½–1 teaspoon dried basil and/or oregano (or dried mixed herbs)
400g can of tuna, drained
salt and pepper (preferably freshly ground)
4 large potatoes (the Forces use instant mashed potato)
splash of milk
knob of butter or margarine
piece of Cheddar or similar cheese (about 75g)

How you do it:

1 Start with the vegetables. If you are using a raw onion, you'll need to peel and cut it in smallish slices or chop it fairly small. If you are following the Forces' recipe to the letter then you need to soak the dried onions for a few minutes, then drain and dry them before moving on. Heat a little olive oil in a frying pan and slowly fry them until they are golden brown.

2 While the onion's cooking, peel and slice the carrots and parboil in a pan of salted water for 6–7 minutes (parboil means 'part boil', which you do when you want to get the cooking started but you plan to finish it another way – in our case by baking in the oven). If using fresh or frozen peas, throw them in after 3 minutes (canned ones don't need parboiling as they're cooked already). Drain the lot and pop them into an ovenproof dish and add the fried onions (add the drained, canned peas, too, now if you are using them). Tip the soup into the dish with the veg and stir in the herbs. Ideally, use chopped, fresh basil but dried is fine and/or some oregano (which are both heavily used in Italian cooking) and finish with a twist of cracked black pepper or just ground pepper, if that's all you have. If you want to make your life easier, you can use a pinch of dried, mixed herbs instead of the basil and oregano but it won't taste so authentic. Now add the drained tuna and set aside while you get the mashed potatoes done.

3   Again, like the dried onion, the Forces use instant mashed potato that you make up with boiling water and a little milk – just follow the pack instructions if you want to go this way – but real mashed potatoes are easy to do. Factor one large potato per person – so four in this instance; it might not sound like enough but when you have mashed them and added milk and a bit of butter or marge they go a long way. Peel the spuds and then cut them up into golf-ball-sized pieces. Getting them roughly the same size is important as that way they

will all be cooked at the same time. Put them in a pan of salted water, bring up to the boil and let them boil for 15–20 minutes. You'll know when they are ready when you can easily slide a fork or knife into the spud chunks. At that point drain them in a colander before returning them to the same pan. Add a splash of milk and a knob of butter or margarine, plus a pinch of salt and pepper, and then mash until you get it to the consistency you like – lumpy or smooth.

4   When the mash is ready, preheat the oven to 180°C/gas 4. Spoon the mash on top of the tuna mix. Keep going until you have covered the lot and then grate a generous amount of cheese all over the top. Pop it into the oven and let it heat through until the cheese and mash on top have gone a lovely golden brown. '*Buon appetito*', as our Italian friends would say.

THE SPECIAL RELATIONSHIP

The UK has a long history of coveting what the US has. (Hell, we even wanted the whole damn continent and everything in it for a while there.) Well it's no different when it comes to Forces food. While, as you have been discovering, the food in the canteens at the British bases is pretty good, it's nothing to what our American cousins get served up. Not only are portion sizes (not surprisingly) considerably bigger, they tend to serve things that no one else gets – like at Camp Phoenix in Afghanistan, where you can get proper surf and turf and BBQ wings and ribs from The Smoke House – a barbecue hut run by the catering guys, which is said to be the best around.

Outside of camp it's the same story – while our twenty-four-hour ration packs are a pretty good mix of three boil-in-the-bag meals, a dessert, a snack and, of course, being British, tea bags, there's plenty of stuff our guys try to steal from the American equivalent. Not only are their ration packs, once again, three or four times bigger than ours, but they also, for instance, contain recognisable name-brand sweets such as M&Ms and Skittles (Brit packs tend to contain generic non-brands).

So the next time you hear a British general saying what an honour it is to serve alongside our American allies, it may have nothing to do with their military might or tactical knowhow but more a chance to get their hands on their grub.

SPICY BEEF BURRITOS

There is no denying the deliciousness of Mexican food – a lip-smacking, mouthwatering scrumptiousness that has seen a huge rise in the popularity of dishes such as Spicy Beef Burritos. (Fact fans among you will delight to hear that 'burrito' is Spanish for 'little donkey', supposedly because the finished product resembles the rolled-up packs the animals carried on their backs.) Yes, damn tasty they may be but you do have to question their suitability in a combat zone.

While the god-like genius of meeting spicy meat, melted cheese and veg in an easy-to-carry tortilla package is undeniable, you do wonder if plying men and women with such treats and their, ahem, well-documented 'after-effects' is such a good idea. Here are brave soldiers putting themselves on the line day in and day out, who often rely on one another for their very lives, now trapped with the self-same people under canvas for hours on end. Have you seen the fireside scene in classic Mel Brooks's comedy *Blazing Saddles*? Would you really be at your best to face Johnny Taliban after being subjected to a night's worth of air biscuits, a handful of gut drops and a smattering of trouser-tuba tuning? We fear not.

So while the contents of Menu Box C contains everything you need to prepare a pan full of these beauties, we do suggest that – unlike the poor, unfortunate soldiers who have no choice – you take to eating these when you have the house to yourself.

You have been warned . . .

> " . . . you will delight to hear that 'burrito' is Spanish for 'little donkey', supposedly because the finished product resembles the rolled-up packs the animals carried on their backs. "

For four servings

You will need:

For the tortillas:
225g plain flour
warm water

For the filling:
splash of olive oil
400g minced beef (the Forces used
    canned minced beef and onions)
salt and pepper
2 garlic cloves, chopped (or
    ½ teaspoon garlic powder)
1 large onion, chopped (the Forces
    use rehydrated dried onion)
400g can of red kidney beans,
    drained
400g can of chopped tomatoes
good chunk of Cheddar cheese,
    grated
hot chilli sauce to taste

How you do it:
1 Start by making the tortillas that the lovely burrito filling will be encased in. You can, of course, buy them pre-made from supermarkets but, for the authentic Forces approach, we're going to make them ourselves. First things first: make a dough from the flour and water. Pile the flour on a work surface, create a little well in the middle and slowly add warm water to it until it starts getting to the consistency of Play-Doh. Keep

adding water if it's too stiff or flour if it's too runny.
2 When you are happy with the dough, divide it into balls and roll them out so they become 20cm discs, roughly the same size as a small dinner plate. (You can of course put an actual plate onto the dough and cut around it and repeat until you have as many as you need.)
3 Next, put a dry frying pan that can comfortably cook each tortilla flat – so one that is bigger than 20cm diameter –

over a moderate heat. When hot, quickly toast each tortilla for a minute or two on each side. Don't put any oil or butter in the pan – you need to cook them 'dry'; and don't overcook them, either, as they will go hard and crispy, and you won't be able to fold them around the filling. Wrap them in foil or a cloth once cooked to keep them soft while you carry on with the rest of the recipe.

4   With the filling you can go one of two ways. Route one is the authentic Forces method. As all of their ingredients in Menu Box C are already cooked or part-cooked, they just mix the whole lot together, spoon it into the tortillas, roll them up, pop in a greased tin, sprinkle with a little extra cheese and bake at 190°C/gas 5 for 20–25 minutes.

5   For those wanting a little more cooking experience, here's what you'll need to do. Heat a little olive oil in a large frying pan and chuck in the minced beef. As it cooks, add a little salt, pepper and the garlic and give it a good mix. As the beef begins to brown, add the chopped onion and cook for a

> **"** . . . the god-like genius of meeting spicy meat, melted cheese and veg in an easy-to-carry tortilla package. **"**

few minutes until the meat is crumbly, not lumpy, before adding the drained kidney beans, the can of chopped tomatoes, and handful of grated cheese. Bring up to the boil, turn down the heat a bit and, once it is merrily blipping away, add in a heap more cheese and the chilli sauce – add a little or a lot, the amount depends on how much you like the heat. Allow the mixture to bubble away for a bit and for it to reduce down so that it isn't too runny when you come to spoon it onto the tortillas, which would just soak through and make for a very sloppy snack: 10 minutes or so should do the trick.

6   When you are happy with the consistency, take it off the heat and allow to cool a little. Line a baking dish with foil and oil the foil. Preheat the oven to 190°C/gas 5. Spoon the beef mixture onto the tortillas. Aim to plop a good dollop into the centre of each disc before rolling up to form your burritos and placing them side by side in the dish. Once they are packed in like commuters in a 7 a.m. train carriage, grate a little more cheese on top and bake in the oven for 20–25 minutes. When the cheese has melted and is golden brown, tuck in.

MELTED CHEESE SPAMCAKES

Some dishes are special: they are cooked to mark a momentous occasion like a twenty-first birthday or a wedding anniversary. They usually take a lot of effort, a lot of time and a helluva lot of ingredients. And then – at the other end of the foody spectrum – lies 'comfort food'. No less important nor delicious but decidedly, and unapologetically, guaranteed to put a smile on your face. And where makes more sense to eat a dish that brings you comfort than when you're hundreds of miles away from home having bullets fired at your head? This tasty snack is widely made and eaten by today's Forces and comes from the ingredients in Menu Box C.

> " comfort food . . . decidedly, and unapologetically, guaranteed to put a smile on your face. "

For four servings

You will need:

1 large onion (the Forces use rehydrated dried onion)
splash of olive oil
340g can of Spam
4 large potatoes for mashing (the Forces instant mashed potato)
salt and pepper
pinch of dried mixed herbs
splash of milk
knob of butter or margarine
good chunk of Cheddar (or similar) cheese
vegetable or sunflower oil for frying

How you do it:

1   Start by prepping the onions. The Forces make use of dried onions that need to be soaked as per the packet directions and then drained and dried on kitchen paper. If you are going this authentic way then please keep some of the drained, flavoured water for use later. If you are using a fresh onion, then peel it before chopping it into smallish cubes or slices (you don't have to be too precise here – just get them to a size you are happy to tuck into when you have your finished Spamcake) and fry them in a little olive oil, over a gentle heat, until they are golden brown. This should take about 10 minutes and will leave the onions tasting sweet and lovely. Pop the onions – whichever method you employed – into a mixing bowl and put to one side while you set about the Spam.

2   You can, of course, use any canned meat for this dish – corned beef, chicken, ham, luncheon meat – but if you are wondering what the Army uses, it's our old friend, Spam. Get the meat out of the tin and chop it into similar-sized pieces to the onion and add it to the bowl. Give it a stir and then crack on with the mashed spuds.

3   The Forces, once again, have to use a powdered ingredient which, among other things, is obviously a much quicker way of getting your grub to the all-important eating stage. If you are using instant mash then simply add the contents of a four-servings packet into the bowl containing the meat and onions and give it a good stir. Add in a little water (the flavoured, drained onion water if you used dried onions, but normal boiled water is fine too) and get the ingredients to a consistency where you will be able to mould it into your desired shape (think plasticine and you won't go far wrong). Then add a pinch of dried mixed herbs and stir it through again. If you are using fresh spuds for the mash then peel them and cut them up into golf-ball-sized pieces. Getting them roughly the same size is important, as that way they will be cooked at the same time. Put them in a pan of salted water, bring to the boil and let them boil for 10–15 minutes. You'll know when

they are ready when you can slide a fork or knife into the spud chunks easily. At that point drain them in a colander before returning them to the same pan. Add in a splash of milk and a knob of butter or margarine, plus a pinch of salt and pepper, and then mash until you get it to the consistency you like. Once you have got to this point, repeat the instructions above – namely, add the mash to the meat and onion in the bowl and give it a good stir together along with a pinch of mixed herbs.

4   Now tip the lot onto a clean, floured work surface (a light dusting of flour helps ensure the mixture doesn't stick to the top you are working on) and mould it into thin disc-shaped patties – 1cm thick is ideal as it won't take long to cook – and then put them on a grill rack, brush with a little oil and grill them under a medium heat, turning them once or twice until golden brown on both sides. You can of course fry them instead. Pour some oil in a frying pan until you have a thin layer just covering the base of the pan (you don't need any more as you are only shallow-

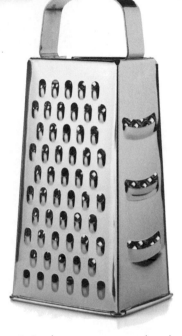

frying). Set the pan over a medium heat and, when hot, carefully pop the patties in, turning them over after a few minutes so they are golden brown on both sides, then remove and drain them on some kitchen paper.

5   Finally, finish the patties off with a good dollop of melted cheese – to do this, put them all on a tin-foil-lined baking tray, grate cheese on top of each patty (put as much as you want on) and then pop the lot under a medium-hot grill until the cheese melts.

PEACH FLAN AND CUSTARD

It is often said that boys never really grow up – it's just the toys get more expensive. Well, that is certainly true of the British Army, especially when you consider their new state-of-the-art spying gear – the Black Hornet Nano – which is little more than a mini, remote-controlled toy helicopter. Since 2012, we Brits have been using the Nano out in Afghanistan to spy on Johnny Taliban. Its tiny size (it measures only 10 x 2.5cm) and huge range (it can fly for half a mile at a top speed of 22 m.p.h.) helps keep soldiers safe by relaying everything they see via a tiny video camera to an operative safely back at base. The self-same can be said of this entry into the canon of army food,

as it's, essentially, a grown-up version of a comforting kids' pud and all made from the ingredients from Menu Box C.

For four servings

You will need:

For the pastry:
125g plain flour
pinch of salt
1 handful of porridge oats
60g margarine (you can use butter for a better taste but the Army uses marge)
2–3 tablespoons cold water

For the filling:
400g can of sliced peaches in syrup, drained keeping the juice
50g mixed dried fruit
granulated sugar
jar of apricot jam
instant custard

How you do it:
1 First make the pastry. Put the flour, salt and oats into a bowl and give them a good mix. Then add in the margarine or butter and use your fingers squish it all together – keep going until you have something that resembles coarse breadcrumbs. Next, stir in just enough cold water to bind these big breadcrumbs together. Don't add all 3 tablespoons in one go, just a little at a time, and stop when the pastry is still a little crumbly (you don't want to go too far and for it to become all elastic and soft). When you get to this stage, wrap the dough in clingfilm and chill in the fridge for at least 10–15 minutes before moving on to the next stage. (You can leave it overnight if you have the time.)

> **"** . . . it's, essentially, a grown-up version of a comforting kids' pud . . . **"**

2 When the pastry is chilled, it's time to 'blind-bake' it. This doesn't mean continuing the recipe while wearing a blindfold (ho ho) but means part-baking the crust before you throw the filling in, which stops the soggy peaches from seeping through the pastry. Preheat the oven to 200°C/gas 6, then take the pastry from the fridge and roll it out on a lightly floured surface (it stops it from sticking). When you have it big and wide enough, gently lay it on the top of a 18–20cm flan dish or sandwich tin you'll be cooking the dessert in. Don't worry if it splits when you are doing it – just patch it up as you go along. Next, lay a sheet of greaseproof paper on top of the pastry and then on top of that add some dried peas, lentils or beans, which will hold the pastry in place and prevent it puffing up when you cook it. Place in the oven and bake for 10 minutes. Take it out and remove the peas/lentils/beans and greaseproof paper and pop the flan back in the oven for 5 minutes to just firm up the bottom. When time is up, remove the flan and set it to one side to cool a bit.

3 Once the pastry is getting towards room temperature, move on to the filling. First up, smear the inside of the pastry all over with plenty of the apricot jam. Next, chop up the canned peaches and mix with a little splash of the reserved syrup and the mixed fruit and then gently spoon the lot into your pastry case. Finally, sprinkle sugar all over the top for a nice crunchy caramelised topping and then bake in the oven for 20–25 minutes. Serve with instant custard and enjoy.

CHICKEN AND POTATO CAKE ON A PEA PURÉE

The world of rarified haute cuisine – of jus, snail porridge and supping sea-flavoured foam while listening to crashing waves on a pair of headphones (no, this *really* happens) – might seem a long way from a mess hall in Afghanistan. But being under combat conditions is no barrier to producing fine dining. Take this recipe, for example. Made from the contents of Menu Box A, this wouldn't look out of place being served in the restaurants of a Heston, Gordon or Jamie. And for those of you reading this who are instantly scared off by cordon-bleu-style cooking and terms such as 'pea purée' think of this more as a big fritter and fancy mushy peas.

There are two ways to cook the cakes so please pick the version you are more comfortable with. The first more closely follows the Forces' recipe and is the simpler of the two. The second uses more fresh ingredients, takes a little longer and is a wee bit more involved (but by no means intimidating or difficult to do).

For four servings

You will need:
450g diced chicken (the Forces use 2 x 400g cans of chicken in white-wine sauce)

1 onion (the Forces use rehydrated dried onion)

500g potatoes for mashing (the Forces use instant mashed potato)

200g porridge oats

300g fresh or frozen peas (the Forces use canned – you'll need a 550g can)

margarine or butter

splash of vegetable or sunflower oil

salt and pepper to taste

How you do it:

1 Preheat the oven to 140°C/gas 1. If doing the Forces way, drain the cans of cooked chicken in sauce so you are left with just the flavoured meat and put it in a mixing bowl with the instant mashed potato and the rehydrated onions (both just require reinvigorating with the requite amount of boiling water and left to soak). Give them a good stir together, then shape the mixture into 4 potato cakes (discs approximately 3cm thick and 10–12cm wide) and then roll each in the oats for a nice crunchy coating. Shallow-fry each cake in margarine for about 4 minutes on each side or until they are a nice golden colour all over, then pop them in the oven to keep warm while you make the pea purée (see stage 5 on page 90).

2 The second way to cook the potato cakes starts with boiling your spuds. Peel them, chop them up into golf-ball-size pieces. Put them in a pan of salted water, bring to the boil and boil for 15–20 minutes or until they're soft enough to mash.

3 While they are bubbling away, we're going to cook the chicken. Fry it off in a little oil, butter or margarine until cooked through, stirring so it doesn't burn, and add a little salt and pepper to taste. The easiest way to check if it's cooked is to fish a couple of the thickest pieces of chicken out of the pan and cut in half. If they are cooked all the way through and there are no signs of pink, then you are good to go. Remove them from the pan with a slotted spoon and put it into a bowl. Next, add the chopped onion to the pan and cook it until it's just soft and golden (adding a tiny bit more oil, if necessary). Take it off the heat. Now we need to chop up the chicken into smaller pieces before mixing it with the fried onions.

> 66 For those . . . scared off by cordon-bleu-style cooking and terms such as 'pea purée', think of this more as a big fritter and fancy mushy peas. 99

4 When the spuds are cooked (when you can stick a fork or knife through them easily), drain them in a colander and tip back into the pan. Mash them with a little margarine or butter. Then to the mash: mix in your chicken and onion, and season it to taste. Next, divide the lot into four equal balls and shape into the classic potato cake shape. Sprinkle the oats on top of each one and then flip over and sprinkle again, pressing them gently into the surface of the cakes – to give a lovely crunchy texture. Put some butter or olive oil (or a mixture of both) in a frying pan over medium heat. When hot, gently place the cakes into the pan. Cook for 2–3 minutes on each side and then pop in the oven to keep warm while you make your pea purée.

5 For the pea puree, if using fresh or frozen peas, pop them into a pan of boiling salted water for 5 minutes or so until tender. Drain them in a colander, then return to the pan. Alternatively, just heat the canned peas in a saucepan, then drain and tip them back in the pan. Using a hand-held blender, purée them to create a smooth paste. If you don't have a blender, tip them in a food processor, and if you don't have a food processor just mash them in a bowl with the back of a fork. If you want a very fine purée, after blending by your chosen method, push the mixture through a fine sieve before serving. (If this takes you a long time, you may need to pop it back in a saucepan to heat through, while stirring so it doesn't burn).

6 Spoon the purée onto serving plates and spread out a little. Pop a chicken cake on top of each, and, as a French gentleman with a pencil-thin moustache would say in a fancy restaurant, '*bon appetit.*'

PROPER PRACTICE PREVENTS PISS-POOR PERFORMANCE

The winners of TV reality cooking competitions like *Masterchef* or *Great British Bake Off* would have you believe that the months of cooking they have just been through are some of the most difficult and stressful of their lives. While that may be the case for the retired accountants from Wakefield, or housewives from Pinner, it is small (food-based pun alert) beans compared with the competitions that the Forces run to keep their chefs in tiptop condition.

Every year a Culinary Challenge is organised across all of the three arms of the British Forces – Army, Navy, Air Force – to see who can be the best of the best in a series of different competitions. Right from the off, the Forces contest is a much more demanding one as the chefs often have to build their own kitchens and cookers from scratch. Against the clock, soldiers can find themselves having to spend an hour digging through hard chalk in order to make an oven pit, construct work surfaces, and collect firewood and water to cook with before they can even open a tin or peel a spud. You don't see John Torode or Mary Berry forcing their lot to do that.

The fact that the food prepared does not suffer in quality is also testament to the abilities of our Forces chefs – winning entries from years past include knocking

> **“** … what real cooking under pressure is all about. **”**

up a chicken stuffed with rabbit, partridge and liver pâté as well as an apple strudel with sauce anglaise: all from a basic, shared larder of ingredients which contains many of the items used in this chapter's recipes.

All of which has given us an idea for how they could improve these TV cooking shows. The next time some ruddy-cheeked IT consultant from Leeds breaks down in tears because their soufflé has failed to rise, Greg Wallace should emerge dressed in full camouflage, barking sergeant-major-like, as he drags him and the other contestants onto a waiting Hercules transport plane which flies non-stop to Iraq, before dumping them in a desert, handing them a spade and a ten-man ration pack and telling them to start again. Only then would you get to see what real cooking under pressure is all about.

CALZONE

It may sound like a toilet-cleaning product or some football-analysing software, but calzone is actually the Italian for Cornish pasty. While that's not strictly true (or indeed true at all), the two do look exceedingly similar and they were created for the same reason – eating on the go. A fact that contributes to this dish being hugely popular in Forces canteens the world over – if meal time is interrupted by a need to go out on operation, dinner doesn't have to be left behind.

The calzone starts life as a humble pizza, which then gets folded in half and has its edges sealed before being cooked (hence looking just like our very own pasty). Like bubble and squeak, the calzone is also a great depositor for leftover ingredients – another reason why it's so popular with the Forces, who aim not to waste a thing. Great served hot or cold, this cracking recipe is pulled together from Menu Box C.

For six servings

You will need:

For the dough:
1kg flour plus extra for dusting
2 x 7g sachets of fast-action dried yeast
2 teaspoons garlic powder
about 600ml luke-warm water

For the filling:
olive oil
100g minced beef (the Forces use canned minced beef and onion)
2 large onions (the Forces use rehydrated onion)
400g can of red kidney beans, drained
2 tablespoons chilli sauce
200g chopped tomatoes (use ½ x 400g can as that's cheaper. The Forces use dehydrated tomato)
salt and pepper
50g cheese, grated

How you do it:

1   First, turn your oven up full whack while you make the pizza dough. Mix the flour, yeast, 1 teaspoon of the garlic powder and the salt together in a large bowl and gradually add the luke-warm water a little bit at a time. You need to mix it in well as you are aiming to end up with a soft, pliable dough. When that's done, dump the dough out onto a floured work surface and knead it for about 5 minutes until it's smooth and elastic. Transfer the doughy lump to a clean bowl and cover it with a damp tea towel and then leave it in a warm place for 1½ hours so that the dough can double in size.

2   While it is rising, make the filling. The quickest way – and it's the Forces way – is to bung the rest of the ingredients in a bowl, season with salt and pepper and then mix together. (If you're using army-style dehydrated onion then you'll have to pre-soak them in boiling water for 5 minutes before draining and adding them to the bowl. Remember to drain your kidney beans too.) If you want to go this way it's not a problem: just skip the rest of this paragraph, but for a bit more 'cooking' before you get to the baking, read on. Pour a splash of olive oil into a hot frying pan. Add the mince and chopped-up onions, toss briefly in the hot oil before adding the rest of the garlic powder, the chilli sauce and some salt and pepper. Fry for a few minutes, stirring, until the meat is broken up and crumbly, not lumpy, before adding in the drained kidney beans, chopped tomatoes and some salt and pepper. Stir it all together and allow to bubble for about 5 minutes – what you're aiming for is to simmer away some of the liquid till you're left with a thickish mixture that's not too 'wet' as it will soak in and ruin the dough. When you are happy with the consistency, take it off the heat and leave it to cool.

3 After the dough has risen, it needs to have the excess air knocked out of it, a process unsurprisingly called 'knocking back'. To do this, scoop the dough out of the bowl and pop it on a lightly floured surface (it might help

> **"** The calzone starts life as a humble pizza, which then gets folded in half and has its edges sealed before being cooked . . . **"**

to have flour on your mitts too to stop anything sticking), then knead the dough for a few minutes until it starts to look as it did before it was left to rise (soft, smooth and elastic). When it's back to this stage, divide the dough into six balls and roll each out onto a lightly floured work surface until about the thickness of a pound coin. These are the calzone bases.

4 At this stage, preheat the oven to 240°C/gas 8. Divide the cooled filling evenly between the calzones and spread it out over half of each doughy base, leaving a gap around the edge

so you can seal the calzone and not have a load of meaty sauce spilling out. Top each filling with a little grated cheese. Dampen the edge of the dough with water. Carefully lift one edge of the dough and pull it over towards the other to effectively fold the calzone in half. Pinch the edges together well so none of the filling can come out (for a more professional-looking finish you can also crimp them with a fork). Place the calzone on 1 or 2 floured baking sheets and bake in the very hot oven for 10–15 minutes or until the dough is puffed up and golden brown.

CHAPTER 3

Bug Banquets, Snake Steaks and Iranian Mars Bars

Like us civvies, the vast majority of serving men and women never have to think about truly fending for themselves. Even when they're away from base for days at a time the trusty twenty-four-hour ration packs go with them. But every so often things go terribly wrong. They are cut off from supplies, the packs run out and they have to catch, kill and cook their own food. Of course, there is another breed of soldier for whom this is an everyday occurrence. The likes of the breathtakingly brave SAS regularly place themselves in harm's way miles from a mess hall, a Greggs or, even, a single, solitary Egg Banjo. For these guys living off the land is an essential part of their training. In this chapter you'll learn a little bit of what it's like to have to get your own grub and live off bugs, birds and bits of bark.

BUG BANQUET

There are many unsavoury things the modern-day soldier has to overcome. Getting shot at, never showering alone and using a hole in the ground as a latrine being just three. Handling that little lot means it's safe to say today's Forces are no place for the faint-hearted – which is fortunate because, in a survival situation, there is nothing more likely to get the stranded soldier through his or her predicament than chowing down on handfuls of creepy-crawlies. Sounds unappetising we know (and don't worry: not everything in this chapter is so unappealing), but insects have a lot going for them. They're your most reliable source of food as they can be found everywhere on the planet, they don't take a lot of effort or ingenuity to catch and what they lack in size they make up for in quantity. And, as if that wasn't enough, in a survival situation they have more nutritional value weight for weight than vegetables – being high in fat, protein and carbs.

Insects can be life-savers, then, but if you're not a member of Her Majesty's Forces, you need to overcome any squeamishness pretty darn fast. If it helps, consider the humble prawn. They're eaten every day, are widely loved but are really nothing more than sea insects. Don't believe me? Well just look at the facts. If something scuttled out from under a flower pot that looked like a prawn, with their multitude of legs, their body armour and their weird, elongated antennae you'd be reaching for the nearest shoe to dispense some bug-splatting justice. Yet just because they turn a nice pink colour when they are cooked and go so very well with Thousand Island dressing, we can't stop tearing off their heads, peeling off their legs and scoffing the whole lot down . . . That's the way you need to think of insects.

Assuming, then, that you are prepared to get stuck in and give this dish a go, you'll be happy to know your Bug Banquet can be made up of anything – ants, grasshoppers, caterpillars, crickets, worms – whatever you can most readily get your hands on. As a rule of thumb the only insects to avoid are those that are brightly coloured (the bright colours are a defence mechanism to warn bigger creatures – that is you – that they are poisonous), that smell bad (again, a sign they will probably give you the squits at best and a small dose of death at worst) or have a sting or bite on them. In this last case – as with some ants – you can still eat them, just take more care in the catching and cooking of your meal.

So to sum up – insects may look weird but they could save your life and it can't be any worse than eating a deep-fried Mars bar, can it? Yes, Scotland, we're looking at you . . .

You will need:
as many of your chosen insect or
    insects as you can gather
matches or fire-making equipment.
water
pot or container to boil them in

How you do it:
1   Before you start, if you are going to
have a crack at this recipe and you're
not in an actual life-threatening situation,
and more importantly don't want to be
plunged into one, then it's probably best
to warn your other half that you intend to
dig around your garden like a three-year-
old, before bringing everything you find
into the kitchen. In fact, it might be best
to wait until they are out the house for
a few hours or, better still, a few days
before giving this a go.
2   Okay, on to the cooking. There's
a couple of ways you can go about
eating your bugs. If you're still feeling
a bit bilious about it all, then the most
palatable way to eat insects and still get
all the attendant nutrition is to pop them
into an empty pot sitting over a hot fire

to dry them out. (If you are actually
stranded in the middle of nowhere
without a pot, then on top of a big stone
placed in the fire will work just as well.)
When they have been roasted like this
for 10 minutes or so, grind them down
until they form a powder or paste, which
can be eaten straightaway or mixed with
other food to make it easier to deal with.
3   If you are feeling braver, then the
most sensible way to prepare your bugs
is to boil them
in water for
a few minutes
before eating. This
has the triple action
of destroying any bacteria
or poison they contain, making
them more palatable to eat and will
aid in helping you remove any hairs
(on caterpillars) or armour (on beetles
and the like) before chomping on the
nutritional insides.
4   Of course if you are
feeling totally SAS-level brave
and want to maintain as much
of the nutrition from your bounty

as possible, then the best way to eat
them is raw. I know that's a lot to take
on board but just think – if namby-pamby
pampered celebrities can do it in the
jungles of *I'm a Celebrity . . . Get Me
Out of Here*, then big, tough wannabe
soldiers should have no problem.
Whichever way you choose to eat your
bugs, once you overcome the idea of it,
they can be tasty, nutritional and, most
importantly, life-saving.

CEVICHE

Ceviche is, basically, a way of 'cooking' fish with the citric acid found in fruits like lemons and limes. No one is entirely sure where it originated but you can find it being served all over Spain and throughout most Latin American countries. The other thing you need to know about ceviche is it tastes amazing. So, while you might have thought survival eating would be all dirt sandwiches with a side-order of bark and moss, ceviche is here to show you it's not all bad.

The reason a dish usually found on upmarket menus is taught to soldiers as part of survival training is that, as well as being easy to do and requiring very few ingredients and no cooking equipment, it can be mixed together and carried with them in a sealed container, merrily marinating ready to be eaten later in the day. That makes this ceviche the ideal endurance fast food.

You will need:

250g very fresh fish, filleted and skinned (you can use practically anything – salmon, cod, plaice, tuna. As a rule of thumb, if it can be eaten raw in sushi it works, so stay away from the likes of prawns)

3 limes, lemons or oranges (whichever you prefer or, in the wild, whichever is growing)

These next ingredients are optional extras as they obviously wouldn't be readily available in a survival situation, but they do help turn the flavour dials in this dish up to eleven:

1 onion or shallot, finely chopped
1 fresh green chilli, deseeded and finely sliced or chopped
pinch of salt
1 handful of fresh coriander

How you do it:

1 Slice the fish as thinly as you possibly can and then put the strips in a bowl. Squeeze your limes (or lemons or oranges) all over it and, if you have chosen to use the extra ingredients, throw in the onion, chilli and a little salt.

2 Gently but thoroughly, mix the ingredients together, so all the fish is well coated in juice and then cover the bowl with clingfilm or a plate and leave it to marinate for at least an hour or until the fish turns opaque (3–4 hours is perfect), or up to 12 hours, if you have the time. Basically, the citric acid in the juice will 'cook' the fish and leave it tasting amazing and fresh. Just before serving, chop the coriander leaves and serve over the top.

3 If you want a more authentic 'survival' version, then fridges and coriander are out, so simply take your fish and cover it with the juice. Leave as above to 'cook' in as cool or shaded a spot as you can find and then eat. Ray Mears eat your heart out . . .

NIL BY MOUTH

While it may seem a little extreme, there are experiments going on right now to see if it is possible to survive without any food or water at all. And not just for a matter of days either: we're talking about decades. Since 2010, military medics have been studying a gentleman by the name of Prahlad Jani, an Indian yogi who claims to have spent the last seventy-odd years getting by without any sustenance whatsoever.

The spiritual soul is under twenty-four-hour observation at a hospital in the western Indian city of Ahmedabad to ensure he isn't sneaking an occasional Mars bar when no one is looking. The military are hoping that by monitoring him and measuring his brain and heart activity they can find out how it is possible to sustain the human body without ingesting anything. Clearly the results could pave the way to not just helping soldiers' survival techniques, but also victims of natural disasters and even astronauts heading off on long-distance missions to the moon and beyond.

The yogi claims to have developed his powers after being visited by a goddess when he was a child who bestowed upon him the ability to use meditation to get by without grub. How practical this is to the modern military is yet to be ascertained but if, in the future, we are confronted with the sight of soldiers sitting cross-legged, repeating a transcendental meditation mantra on the battlefield then we know Prahlad Jani has come up trumps.

PINE-NEEDLE TEA

> ❝ . . . a cup of the soon-to-be-described pine-needle tea has as much vitamin C as a glass of orange juice . . . ❞

Think of the humble pine tree and you are likely to be transported by images of twinkling fairy lights on an immaculately decorated Christmas tree. However, for the British Army and other assorted survivalists, the tree is known as a potential source of nutrition and medicine and, in extreme situations, can even be a life-saver. The reason for these wild-sounding claims can be found in the tree's pine needles (and, actually, their inner, soft bark and sap are pretty good too). Not only are the spiky leaves good for decorating the carpet and sticking in the soles of your feet throughout the month of December and late into January, they also happen to be seriously high in both vitamin A and vitamin C. In fact, a cup of the soon-to-be-described pine-needle tea has as much vitamin C as a glass of orange juice and five times the amount you find in a lemon. There is a lot of research suggesting that people have survived on pine-needle tea as their only source of nutrition for days on end, as well as downing it in less life-threatening scenarios to keep diseases, like scurvy, at bay. (Over in the US, communities of Native Americans have been glugging down a version of this tea for years, believing that not only will it sort out various health problems but it also allows them to obtain the spirit-power of the tree itself.)

Tea isn't the only way of getting the best out of the branchy wonder. Assuming you can't be bothered to make a cuppa – and that would be taking laziness to a whole different level – you can also get nutrition from chewing the needles and swallowing the produced juice. They are especially good to chomp on in the spring when the needles are new, but this method doesn't make much of a recipe: 'Pick. Put in mouth. Chew thoroughly. Swallow the juice. Spit out

the rest.' So we'll stick with making tea. A word of warning, before you boil your kettle, though. Evergreen teas should be used in moderation as large amounts can give you the trots – the high levels of vitamin C can be difficult to digest and so a bellyache and the 100m dash to the loo are to be expected. Also, should you find yourself to be both stranded miles from anywhere *and* pregnant, then, perhaps, check out one of the other recipes in this chapter as it's particularly toxic to those 'with child'. Also, we should point out, for health and safety reasons, that three species of these evergreens are poisonous: yew (which most people recognise as being big, rounded trees, with distinctive red berry-like cones), Norfolk Island pine (which is a relative of the monkey puzzle tree, with wide-apart symmetrical branches) and ponderosa pine (with very long tufted needles and reddish-brown bark), so avoid at all costs.

But in small doses pine-needle tea is fine, and let's be honest: when you are out in the wilderness with nowt else to consume, it could save your life.

For one serving

You will need:
1 handful of young pine needles
water for boiling
1 teaspoon of sugar, honey or maple syrup
stick of cinnamon, a pinch of nutmeg or a slice of orange peel (these extra ingredients would not appear in military training books as most are hard to come by in a survival situation but they will add extra flavour and sweetness, so feel free to add as many or as few as you desire)

How you do it:
1 Snip or pick the needles from the pine and give each of them a little crush between finger and thumb to break the surface and open them up. Or, if you prefer, roughly chop them.
2 While you are doing that, boil a mugful of water and when it's bubbling away, throw in the needles and remove from the heat. Cover and leave for at least 20 minutes but you can leave overnight for a really intense taste.
3 When that's done your tea should be a reddish colour (though, depending on the species, it may be pale green or golden), and a small amount of oil will have risen to the top, which you can skim off if you prefer. Strain the needles from your tea and add sweetener or other flavouring of choice and swig away.

WELCOME TO THE JUNGLE

The recipes detailed in this chapter, while being authentically military, are pretty much designed to be stopgap options only. They're to get soldiers through a tricky couple of days or weeks before, hopefully, being rescued (or, in our case, to provide a bit of fun in the kitchen of a weekend). What no one could imagine is surviving off the land for not just days, weeks or even months, but decades. Yet this is exactly what happened with two WWII Japanese soldiers. Back in the 1970s, Shoichi Yokoi and Hiroo Onoda were discovered on different Pacific islands after living in the wild for twenty-eight and thirty years respectively. Each had been following the last order they were given by their generals: do not surrender. While their tenacity and loyalty is, undoubtedly, admirable, their steadfast refusal to come out of hiding is incomprehensible – especially considering both found out during their self-imposed exiles that the war had, in fact, been over for many years. Still, their experiences give us the following five golden rules for surviving on your own for very long periods of time indeed:

1   You can't be picky when it comes to diet and must eat whatever you can get your hands on – whether you like the food or not. They survived on fruit, nuts, grubs, snails and, even, rats. They both also agreed that obtaining enough to eat, day in and day out, was the single hardest task.

2   When it comes to water, even if seemingly fresh H_2O is abundantly available to you, always boil it up just in case.

3   Be careful what you wish for. It's not hard to imagine that a diet of bugs and dust would have any stranded man or woman constantly dreaming of a nice bacon sandwich.

> **"You can't be picky when it comes to diet and must eat whatever you can get your hands on . . ."**

On examination both men were discovered to have suffered no dental problems whatsoever. They were also in excellent all-round physical and mental health (beyond a spot of malnutrition).

So there you have it: proof that it is possible to survive for decades at a time without mobile phones, *The X Factor* and working in an office. Sounds heavenly.

Well, in particular, Yokoi had reason to regret such fantasies when he came across a wild pig one day. The excitement of catching and killing something so new to his diet soon wore off when he realised how much of the meat was going to waste. Sadly, the bad news doesn't end there as his first meal of pig made him incredibly sick and nearly killed him – the reason being, he was so unused to such big chunks of meat that he didn't cook it for long enough and poisoned himself.

4   Don't forget the little luxuries. Having all that time on your hands also allows you to learn new tricks. Each of the survivalists 'invented' his own little objects to make life that little bit more bearable. One made what was, to all intents and purposes, a three-piece suit, complete with working buttons, belt loops and pockets. The other invented a working toilet that emptied straight into the river.

5   Finally, surviving in the wild is no obstacle to good oral hygiene.

SPIT-ROASTED WOOD PIGEON

While this recipe sounds quite fancy it's basically 'bird cooked over fire'. And, to be quite honest, it doesn't even have to be wood pigeon, as all of our feathered friends are edible. Some, however, taste better than others. The best for eating are game birds, the sort which wouldn't be out of place served at a Michelin-starred restaurant such as pheasants, grouse and partridge. (Strange to think you could eat as well in a survival situation as you can in a high-class eatery, minus the silver service, the white linen and the excruciatingly expensive bill of course.) At the other end of the spectrum are birds of prey – vultures, eagles and the like – for, quite apart from being the beaky equivalent of the SAS and, therefore, hard to catch and kill, their meat is as tough as old boots and their carcasses are full of disease-carrying parasites.

The other upside of hunting birds is that they nest all over the world from seasides to deserts, from forests to mountain ranges. So, if you were desperate, there would always be one somewhere. Consequently, the problem with birds is not which one to target, nor in finding them: it's catching these feathery foodstuffs. Thankfully, there are more options available than Wile E. Coyote got through in his entire career of failing to capture the Roadrunner. For example, with roosting birds, you can attach a noose to the end of a long pole and pull them down from their branch. For ground-dwelling and flightless birds, you can dig a pit which you cover with foliage to camouflage it, place bait (berries and the like) in the middle of the trap and wait for the birds to fall into your hole. You can even catch birds that fly away – wrap bait around a stone and chuck it in the air, the bird takes the snack and the hidden stone causes an unexpected change in weight and the bird crashes to the ground, where you are waiting to pounce.

So far so good, but once you've caught your bird by fair means or fowl (little bird humour there, apologies!) you need to kill it. We know this is all a little grim but, in a survival situation, needs must.

The most humane way to do so is to dislocate the neck. Done properly, it renders the bird unconscious before it dies. Hold the bird upside down so that

> **"**While this recipe sounds quite fancy it's basically 'bird cooked over fire'.**"**

its head is facing the ground and its feet to the sky, then, with your stronger hand, take the bird's head and pull it down and back in one sharp, quick movement. Expect a lot of thrashing around. Just remember, you are very hungry and this is going to make a very tasty meal indeed.

Next you need to remove the blood. The simplest way is to cut its throat and hang it by the feet and let it all drain out. This should take between five and ten minutes, depending on the size of the feathered creature. When the blood has ceased to drip, it's time to pluck the feathers. This is best done as soon as possible, as a warm-bodied bird will allow the feathers to come off easiest. Put down lots of paper and, preferably, do this outside as feathers have a habit of flying around. There is no real skill – you just pull them out in clumps. Be careful with small birds, though, as the skin tears easily and, as you are going to be cooking over a fire, the skin will help stop it drying out. If you are planning to boil or stew your bird, you can rip off the skin,

feathers and all, which is a lot easier.

That done, next on the list is some rudimentary butchering. Cut off the head and feet, before making an incision from the spot where you cut the throat to its tail. Put your hand inside the bird (We told you this was not for the faint-hearted) and pull out all the innards. You need to get everything out, so you are just left with the meat and bones.

(At this point, we should stress the catching and killing of wild birds in this

country without a licence is illegal. So, if you fancy trying out this recipe you'll either have to go on an organised shoot during the hunting season or get given birds by someone who has (they can't sell them to you). The obvious alternative is to bypass all this and buy one ready-plucked from the butcher or supermarket and just try out the cooking method. You could always camp out in the garden for a day without food first just to make it a bit more authentic.)

For one serving

You will need:
matches or fire-making equipment
1 wood pigeon (or other tasty small
    bird)
salt and pepper
sharp knife
short, sturdy stick to use as a spit to
    roast your bird on

How you do it:
1   First, make a fire and light it as it
needs to get nice and hot before you
start cooking and the flames need to die
down a bit. Next, rig up mounts for the
spit stick to rest on over the fire. This takes
a bit of woodcraft as the stick the bird is
secured on needs to 'sit' on top of two
others so that the bird is approximately
10cm above the fire. (Much like a
barbecue, if you find that the flames are
leaping up and burning the outside of
the pigeon then raise it higher. You are
cooking with the heat of the fire, not the
flames, which will just burn the outside

of the bird and leave the inside raw.)
You need to find a pair of similar-sized
branches that resemble a capital letter
'Y' – think the classic water-divining rod
shape – and position these a suitable
distance apart for the spit stick to rest on
over the flames.
2   Any young and smallish bird can
be spit-roasted from scratch. However,
if you have bagged an older bird or one
that eats carrion (basically, the rotting
flesh of dead animals) you would be
better off boiling them first to kill any
possible bacteria and to make a stringy,
tough old bird into something more
tender and nice to eat. Once you've
boiled (or not), rub salt and pepper
(if you have it) inside and outside the
bird before holding your spit – a sharp,
sturdy stick – and pushing it through
the bird, starting at the tail end, guiding
it through as close to the centre of the
carcass as you can before poking it
back out the neck end.
3   Okay, now comes the cooking.
You need to roast your pigeon for

approximately an hour, turning it all the
time to ensure it is cooked throughout.
This timing is a rough estimate as,
depending on the size of your bird –
and the heat of the fire – it could take
much longer. (Obviously, when cooking
normally, a pigeon can be roasted in
much less time and served really pink
but, outdoors in makeshift conditions,
you can't be too careful, so you need
to cook any bird right through.) The
way to be certain is poke your knife into
the thigh of the bird (the thickest part
and therefore the bit that will take the
longest to cook) and check the colour
of the juices that run out. If they are
clear, then the bird is cooked; if they are
bloody or cloudy, then it needs a little
longer. When you have clear juices your
bird is ready to scoff.

IRANIAN MARS BARS

Eating unpalatable things is not just something that happens in forests, swamps and behind enemy lines. Soldiers both at home and overseas regularly find themselves in a survival situation every time they come face to face with an Iranian Mars bar. For info on this peculiar foodstuff, we turn to the ARRSE website (www.aarse.com) for the final time, where we discovered that the chocolate bars squaddies found in their twenty-four-hour ration packs were actually remnants left over from a whole shipment of choccy treats originally made for the late Shah of Iran way back in the 1970s.

These bars weren't delivered, for reasons never fully explained, and so, rather than end up in the Middle East, they ended up in British soldiers' bellies. You can, apparently, tell if you have hold of a genuine Iranian Mars bar by the particular white bloom that has formed itself around the outer layer of the chocolate. The discolouring and distance travelled did absolutely nothing, unfortunately, to improve the taste. Thankfully, such bars are rare these days and so can be treated like a bit of a delicacy should you find one. An unappetising delicacy, but a delicacy none the less . . .

> 66 Eating unpalatable things is not just something that happens . . . behind enemy lines. 99

FRUIT JELLY

From summer onwards, fruit becomes very important for your trapped-behind-enemy-lines soldier, for the fabulous things about fruit are fourfold. (Try saying that after a few pints). Firstly, it can be found pretty much everywhere in the world in some form or other. From deserts (pretty much all cacti have edible fruit), to tundra (the awesomely named crowberry) and to forests (cherries, blackberries and pretty much everything you'd find in an M&S fruit salad; seriously, if you were to get stranded in a survival situation, hope to do it near a forest). Secondly, fruit is also packed with essential vitamins and minerals to

help keep you healthy even when food is scarce. Thirdly, as an added bonus, fruit is the staple diet of many animals and birds, so find the fruit and you have a chance at nabbing some protein too. And, finally, it can be made into a jelly – or rather a pulp – that will keep much better than fresh fruit and can be taken with you, as this recipe will shortly show.

So important is fruit, you need to make yourself familiar with what's around and, more importantly, what's poisonous. The rule of thumb is, if you don't recognise the fruit in front of you and you want to ensure you don't die from eating it, take it in stages. First thing you do is smell it – if it whiffs of almonds discard it as this is often a sign of a poison. Next, squeeze it and rub whatever comes out on your skin. If it irritates you, chuck it away. Next, place a little on your lips and wait for a reaction. Again, with any irritation throw it away. Finally, chew a bit and if there's no reaction then swallow it. Wait five minutes before eating a little more. If all is well, then you are clear to proceed.

You don't have to be in the middle of a jungle or stuck halfway up a mountain to know that fresh fruit goes off pretty quickly. So, while in a survival situation having plenty to eat after stumbling across a fruit-bearing tree or bush is a good thing; it's not much use in the long term if you are stuck in one place and, therefore, limiting your chance of being rescued. So, in order to make the most of what they have and get on the move again, the Forces are taught to make a jelly out of the excess. Now, clearly, we are not talking about the kind of rabbit-shaped mould of kids' party jelly here but more a thick jam-like substance. How does it work? Well, that means breaking out some science. The reason most fruits can be made into a jelly is that they contain a very important ingredient called pectin. This is a naturally occurring setting agent that is found in all ripe fruit and, when heated, reacts with the acid in the fruit and turns it into jelly. (To illustrate the point, old ladies and those who frequent country fayres, will add powdered or liquid pectin to their jams so that they set more quickly and taste better – though that's less of a concern for us, as this is all about surviving and not impressing the Lady Mayoress with a gooseberry preserve.) The levels of pectin vary from fruit to fruit and that will affect how quickly you can make your jelly – which of course is important if you need to get on the move sharpish because you're being hunted by enemy troops, say, or a particularly hungry bear. Fruits high in pectin include citrusy ones such as lemons, limes and oranges as well as blackberries and apples. Those low in pectin – like strawberry – would need some of these other fruits added to make a jelly work. (Though the chances of being in a survival situation and surrounded by strawberries are remote, unless of course you get stranded on manoeuvres in Wimbledon during tennis fortnight.)

We've given you the survival recipe – which is essentially firm fruit pulp – but you could add some sugar and lemon juice once the fruit is pulpy and let it blip away again for a while to make something which will keep even longer.

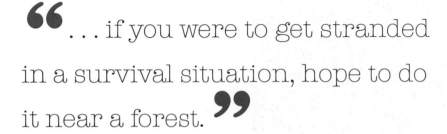

" … *if you were to get stranded in a survival situation, hope to do it near a forest.* **"**

For one or more servings

You will need:
matches or fire-making equipment
as much ripe fruit as you can find
a tin or pan for boiling the fruit in
a container – ideally airtight

How you do it:
1   First make your fire and light it.
2   If possible wash your chosen fruit first, peel off any inedible skin and chop it up if necessary. Tip it in a pot with just a splash of water and gently heat it over a fire. (Obviously if you are using a low-yield pectin fruit you will need to add a few chopped-up apples or the juice of a lemon or whatever you have at this point too.) Stir it

frequently or it will burn. After a while you will see the fruit 'break down' and become mushy – this is essentially your fruit jelly.
3   Once your fruit is boiled, broken down and thick and pulpy, allow it to cool in a safe and clean place, out of direct sunlight and away from any moisture (think rain or dew) as both of these things would mean your jelly spoiling.
4   Once cooled, put it into the cleanest (boil the container and lid in water and only handle when your mitts are at their most clean) and most air-tight container you have, as this will keep it from going off for the longest possible time. You can now get on the move again, safe in the knowledge you have something to chow down on for days to come.

ALTERNATIVE USES FOR RATIONS

The key to success in situations such as we've been discussing in this chapter can be boiled down to the Forces idiom: 'Learn. Adapt. Survive'. Here follow three excellent examples of the ingenuity employed by our bravest and best to utilise the rations they are supplied with in ways entirely unintended by their manufacturers. We can't say they'll improve your chances of survival as a Swiss Army knife would, but they're good for a giggle if nothing else.

Ordnance You met the unlikely-sounding-but-actually-quite-delicious Baby's Head Pudding back in Chapter 1, but the individually canned steak-and-kidney puddings issued in the twenty-four-hour ration packs have another usage – weaponry. Now before we go any further, no one is claiming they can be used to take down a tank or the entire al-Qaeda terrorist network, but they can be, and are, regularly made to explode for humorous purposes. While out on exercise in the dark and cold, morale can be boosted by placing the pudding in its unopened can within a mess tin full of water and heated . . . and heated . . . and heated until the can eventually explodes with spectacular effect and a loud bang, showering any soldiers not fast enough to get away with hot meat and suet crust.

Bunger-Upper While we realise that's not a scientific term, it'll have to do in terms of meaning the opposite of 'laxative'. The 'Bunger-Uppers' in question are the savoury and sweet biscuits supplied in the twenty-four-hour ration packs.

These biscuits, if eaten all at once, are widely acknowledged to have the same desired effect as the kind of instant tablets one takes on holiday to put the brakes on a dose of the Brown Laser.

Machine-gun maintenance and bullet-wound treatment We'll end with a couple that don't utilise food from ration packs, but are just as imaginative and impressive. The use of condoms to keep machine guns firing is a relatively recent 'invention' due to the fact that there are now significantly more desert campaigns. Desert skirmishes naturally mean increased amounts of sand and dust which can get into everything, including rifles, causing them to jam. Clever soldiers stick the rubbers over the muzzles of their machine guns to keep out the worst of it, just firing straight

> " The key to success in situations such as we've been discussing in this chapter can be boiled down to the Forces idiom: 'Learn. Adapt. Survive'. "

through the latex when the time comes. Another personal-protection bit of kit, tampons, have been used for decades by the military to dress wounds. They plug bullet holes really well (especially the deep ones), they absorb a lot of blood, they are completely sterile, have easy-to-use applicators and they leave a tail of cotton behind so they can be easily spotted, removed

and replaced. In fact it's very apt that the humble tampon is used in this way, as the material most often used in them – cellucotton – was originally devised during World War I as a way to improve the absorbency of bandages. It's truly the circle of life. (Though we're not sure that's quite what Elton John had in mind when he was writing *The Lion King . . .*)

SNAKE STEAKS

In the next chapter we'll show you some of the excellent dishes that the great and good of the British Military have enjoyed over the years, including a cracker from ex-SAS soldier and award-winning novelist Andy McNab. However, Andy was generous enough not only to provide his favourite dish from his time in the Forces but also one of his most memorable: a meal which just so happens to be perfect for this chapter on survival eating – boa constrictor steaks. Over to Andy to tell us how this unusual dish came about:

'The Colombian Anti-narcotics Police caught two boas while we were in the rainforest completing a two-week patrol. They gave us one as a gift. The thing was about five foot long. We cut off its head, skinned and gutted it before cutting it into four-inch lengths and cooked it over a fire.

'I remember it had lots of small bones like a fish because, basically, a snake is all spine and ribs. The meat tasted like fish, too, but was meaty like chicken. With some Tabasco splashed onto it while it cooked and a little more to dunk the meat in, it was very good. In fact,

> **"** If anyone was ever in any doubt as to how tough the SAS were, let this be the end of it. **"**

I kept two bits wrapped and had them cold the next day.'

If anyone was ever in any doubt as to how tough the SAS were, let this be the end of it. Eating snakes for fun . . . Legends.

If you're going to follow Andy's lead and eat snake, then you first need to catch and kill a slithery critter. Now, clearly, we are only talking about tackling them in a survival situation as snakes – it won't surprise you to know – can be very dangerous. The rule of thumb here is do not tackle anything bigger than you (sound advice for a Saturday night out too). However, if you find one (and that won't be easy as snakes are fairly awesome at camouflage and avoiding detection) the rest is, actually, quite easy. To dispatch one, the simplest and safest method is to get a forked stick and pin it behind the head before bashing in on the bonce with a bigger stick until it's dead.

If you fancy trying something similar at home, you could buy an eel from your fishmonger and tackle it in the same way.

For one to four servings (depending on size)

You will need:
1 snake
fire-making equipment
sharp knife

How you do it:

1 The first thing you need to do is get a good fire going.

2 Next, tackle the snake. First you need to cut the head off. A good sharp knife will do it, as will a good sharp pair of scissors or shears. If you think you've got a poisonous snake then cut at least 5cm further down the neck to also remove the venom sacks. (Talking of which, don't worry unduly about eating a poisonous snake: cooking it thoroughly will ensure any venom is denatured and rendered harmless.)

3 Next you are going to skin it and to do that you first need to find the charmingly titled 'anal vent' – it's an opening usually found a few centimetres down from the tail. Pop your knife in the vent and slice all the way along the snake towards where the head used to be. Now you've done that you can skin the snake two ways. If you were thinking of fashioning the skin into a nice belt or head band then you need to resort to gently, painstakingly and carefully cutting through the connective tissue between the skin and muscle all the way along the snake's body. The easiest way, however, is to rip the skin off. To do this, you must first separate a centimetre or so of skin from muscle at the head end, and then with a firm grip pull the rest off as if you were peeling a particularly long green banana. (If you have some salt handy, dip your fingers in it first: it gives you a better grip on the skin.) It probably won't come off in one go but, as with a roll of Sellotape, just keep finding the end and carry on till you're done.

4 The final stage is to gut your snake, which is quite easy as all the snake's innards are arranged in a convenient-to-grab tube that runs the length of the body

> **"** … snakes – it won't surprise you to know – can be very dangerous. The rule of thumb here is do not tackle anything bigger than you. **"**

– so just tear it all out. Give the insides a rinse and then it is cooking time.

5 The easiest way to prep the snake for cooking is to chop it into steaks – think salmon steaks – a couple of centimetres thick. (While on the subject of eating – don't forget that snake blood is considered an aphrodisiac among many Asian cultures. That might not be much use to you in a survival situation, stuck as you are on your own in the middle of nowhere, but you might want to save some for your post-rescue celebration. Just a thought.) Once you have your steaks, put a pan on the fire to heat. Bung the steaks into the hot pan and cook for 5 minutes or so on both sides before eating. The good thing to remember here is that all snakes can be eaten; the bad thing is they all taste pretty bland – like a cross between battery-reared chicken and a mild fish. So, if possible, you'll need to follow Andy's lead and splash something like Tabasco over it, to add some full-on seasoning and give the snake steaks a punch. Enjoy.

COKE BOTTLE COD

Having read a few recipes in this chapter, you'll no doubt have picked up on a common thread: that survival eating is all about dishes that are easy to find and easy to catch. It's for that reason, then, that we have another fish recipe, for, unlike land animals, which take outsmarting, trapping and hunting, fish are as dumb as a bag of hair. Thankfully, they taste a whole lot better than hair and contain lots of useful things like protein, vitamins and fish oil, which is thought to help depression – something that could come in handy should you find yourself trapped behind enemy lines. More than that, pretty much all fish you are likely to encounter are edible, so you don't need to know what you are catching (a few have poisonous innards so, if in doubt, clean out).

On reflection, this chapter should, probably, be called 'Pop Bottle Perch' as you are more likely to catch a freshwater perch with this than a thumping big cod from the depths of the ocean but the Coke alliteration rolls off the tongue much better – and you get the drift.

Now you might wonder how the aforementioned low IQ of fish can help you catch them, when anglers the world over will tell you that landing the slippery beggars is an art form, the methods for which are an enigma wrapped in a mystery and cloaked by a riddle. While that may all be true of using the traditional methods of rod and line, you would only try to catch fish that way for 'sport', but we are talking about survival and so all such rules are

 ... survival eating is all about dishes that are easy to find and easy to catch.

out the window. For, assuming they had the equipment, the easiest way to catch fish (freshwater ones at least) is to stretch a net across the narrowest point of the river and scoop up everything that swims your way. However, in a survival situation, you probably don't have a huge net about your person, and you're not Spider-Man and thus able to provide your own, which brings us to this dish and the next easiest method: the Coke bottle trap.

Before getting to the Coke bottle trap, you first need to work out where to fish. The only thing you need to remember here is fish are lazy. Aim for the nicest, safest and most comfortable place to swim and you'll find dinner. In hot conditions go where the water is shady, deep and cool. In cold conditions, go for the shallows where the sun can warm it. If you're by a fast-running river, go where the water is slowest, and so on and so forth.

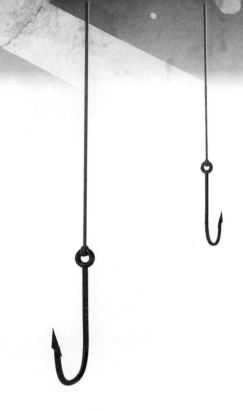

Next, you're going to need some bait to entice your fish into your trap. As a rule of thumb you should use what is around and, therefore, what the fish are, presumably, already eating. The most likely candidates are berries or seeds from nearby plants, or surface-skimming insects or flies. Have a dig around and see what you can find. Of course, failing all that, you can always use the old fisherman's standby of anything shiny (as we said, fish are incredibly stupid).

Now you have your location and your bait you're going to catch them with nothing more than an old plastic drinks bottle. Take the bottle and remove all the labels – you want it to appear as if it is invisible when it is in the water – and then cut all the way through it about 3cm below the neck of the bottle. Now insert the neck 'half' back inside the bottom (i.e. the 'wrong' way round), so it acts like a funnel guiding the fish in. You now have your Coke bottle trap. Deploy it the area you chose earlier using the bait most suited to your spot and you should be catching fish in no time.

When you've secured your dinner, you'll need to kill it quickly and humanely either by a sharp blow to the head with a blunt instrument or by spiking it – running a sharp knife or skewer right in between the eyes. Sorry to sound so brutal but this is about survival.

For one serving

You will need:
matches or fire-lighting equipment
a pan to cook your fish in
and – assuming all goes to plan –
   a fish
look around, you might find some wild
   fennel or garlic to add too

How you do it:
1 Once you've caught something it is on to the cooking. Make a fire and light it. If they are tiddlers (say no more than 5cm in length), just cook and eat them whole. Any bigger than that and you need to do a bit of prep beforehand and it's best to do this as soon as you have caught the fish to maintain the best flavour and to reduce the risk of any bacteria forming.
2 First things first: you need to bleed the fish out – the easiest way is to cut its throat and hang it upside down to let all the blood drain out. While you are doing that, also cut out the gills as these can often harbour a lot of germs. When the

blood has stopped, give the whole fish a rinse over with water and rub off any slime from the skin.

3 Next, set a frying pan (or something similar) over the fire to get really hot.

4 Now you need to gut the fish, so make a slit from where the throat was cut to the hole just above the tail, stick your hand inside and pull out all its guts. (If you think you will be stuck in your situation for a while don't throw the offal away as it can be used for bait next time around.)

5 Next step is de-scaling. Now this isn't vital but if you have the time to do it, it will make for a better eating experience. Lay the fish flat, hold the tail and scrape a sharp knife from its tail up to its head. If you are applying the right amount of pressure you should see scales flying off in all directions. Once you're happy with your descaling, one final step before cooking, which, again, isn't necessary but is an aesthetic one: cut off the head and tail. (If you have found some wild herbs, stuff them in the body cavity now, too.)

6 As you are in a survival situation and fish kettles, lemon juice, butter and assorted herbs and spices are out of reach, the simplest way to cook fish is in that searingly hot pan you set over the fire. The natural oil in the skin will fry it and help keep it moist though the skin may stick to the pan (cleaning is a bit of a pain, so bung it in some water quick when you take the fish out).

7 Lay the cleaned fish in the hot pan, and leave it to cook for 3–5 minutes (depending on the size of the fish). Then carefully turn it over to cook the other side for the same amount of time. Try not to overcook your catch, as dried-out fish is not the greatest. Remove from the heat and get ready to eat, but remember, unlike the fish you get served in the chippy or restaurant, it will still have all its bones intact. So be careful as it would be pretty dumb to choke to death on a stray fish bone after surviving capture and enemy bullets.

CHAPTER 4

Churchill's Stew, Monty's Pudding and Carry On up the Khyber

There have been many remarkable, renowned and recognised men and women who have served in the British Armed Forces over its 300-year history. This chapter concerns just ten of them. We have a recipient of the Victoria Cross, a World Cup winner, an award-winning novelist, as well as more OBEs, MBEs and knighthoods than you can shake a stick at. Each has kindly passed on a meal or recipe that they remember most fondly from their time in the military and we are extremely grateful to them for doing so.

WINSTON CHURCHILL'S VEAL STEW

Sir Winston Leonard Spencer Churchill is widely regarded as one of the greatest wartime leaders ever, and a man who saw Britain through the trials and tribulations of World War II. His steadfast refusal to consider defeat or surrender helped inspire the nation and those fighting both on the home front and overseas. This strength was particularly important in the early days of the war when Britain stood alone in its active opposition to Hitler. Churchill led Britain, and subsequently her allies, through the very darkest of years until victory over Nazi Germany had been secured in 1945. As well as being prime minister, Churchill was also an officer in the British Army, a historian, a writer and an artist. He is the only British prime minister to have received the Nobel Prize in Literature, and was the first person to be made an Honorary Citizen of the United States.

Take one look at any photo of this great man though and you can tell he liked a good meal. Sir Winston Churchill, it is fair to say, knew his way around a menu and, as is deserving of a man who achieved so much, he liked to enjoy the finer things in life. The excellent and

> **"** . . . Hot baths, cold Champagne, new peas and old brandy . . . **"**

exhaustive Churchill Society reports that the man was happy as long as he had 'Hot baths, cold Champagne, new peas and old brandy' to hand, and who would argue with that? He was a well-known fan of the fare served at London's famous Savoy hotel and it is said that the noble establishment still employs staff who cooked for him. He was partial to the Savoy's roast beef and Yorkshire puddings (of course he was, you couldn't get anything more British than that), and was known to prefer a good Stilton to a sweet dessert, but could easily have his arm twisted to have both.

At home, safely ensconced behind the big black door of Number Ten, he was tended to by the Churchill family cook, Georgina Landemare, who was no slouch in the kitchen herself. According to her out-of-print book – *Recipes from Number 10* (Collins, 1958) – one of Winston's favourite dishes was veal stew, the smell of which was enough to make him start imagining members of his war cabinet were dancing slabs of roast meat with apples in their mouths and steam rising from their backs, just like they do in Bugs Bunny cartoons . . . Or, at least, we like to think it did.

For four servings

You will need:

1.5kg stewing veal
225g onions, halved and sliced
1 carrot, diced
1 celery stick, diced
½ leek, diced
1 handful of fresh parsley and
   thyme, chopped, and a couple of
   bay leaves
salt and pepper
1.2 litres chicken stock
225g button mushrooms
splash of vegetable or sunflower oil
40g butter
3 tablespoons plain flour
2 egg yolks
2 tablespoons double cream

How you do it:

1   Cut the veal into small cubes (roughly 2.5cm across but you don't have to be exact – and you can even buy it ready diced from some supermarkets) and then blanch them by dropping the cubes into some boiling salted water for 5 minutes and draining and rinsing them under cold water.

2   When that's done, put the veal, half the onion, all the carrots, celery, leek and the herbs and a good sprinkling of salt and pepper into a large cooking pot along with the chicken stock. Bring to the boil, reduce the heat, pop a lid on it, and let it simmer for 1½ hours. While it's simmering, slice the remaining onions and gently fry with the mushrooms in a splash of oil and when they are softened and starting to brown, remove with a slotted spoon and put to one side.

3   After the 90 minutes, turn the heat right down and remove the meat from the pot and pop it on a plate for a moment. Next, pour the contents through a colander to separate the stock from the veg. You don't want to throw away the stock, so make sure when you strain it that you do so over another pot. Discard the bay leaves. Return the veg to the pot and throw in the butter to melt. When it has, take the pot off the heat and stir in

the flour – this will thicken the lovely juices that are in there. Once it's all mixed together, gradually stir the stock back in, whack up the heat and boil for 2 minutes, stirring all the time so it doesn't go lumpy. Then add in the previously cooked mushrooms and onions and replace the meat. Simmer once more for 7–8 minutes.

4   While it's bubbling away, whisk the egg yolks and cream together until well blended. (The easiest way to separate your egg yolks is to crack the egg in half and then pour the contents back and forth between the two eggshells allowing the egg white to drop away into a dish.) Take the pot off the heat, pour in the yolks and cream mixture, give it a good old stir-up – to enrich and thicken the stew but do it off the heat as you don't want it to boil again or it will curdle. Taste, and add some more salt and pepper if needed. Serve steaming hot in big bowls with some chopped parsley on top. Take that, Jerry.

" . . . imagining members of his war cabinet were dancing slabs of roast meat with apples in their mouths . . . **"**

WHO KNEW?

There are many famous men who have served their countries. There are those, like the first president of the United States, George Washington; hip-swinging, teen-troubling troubador Elvis Presley; or the founder of the Boy Scouts, Robert Baden-Powell, that aren't that surprising. Then there are those who straight-up smack you in the face with shock to find out they ever served. Here are some such examples:

Jimi Hendrix   Guitar legend Jimi spent two years in the US military training to become a paratrooper.

Sir Matt Busby   One of Manchester United's greatest-ever managers was a sergeant major in the Liverpool King's Regiment.

M. C. Hammer   Excessive pantaloon wearer and rapper who spent three years in the US Navy.

Arnold Schwarzenegger Served in the Austrian Army, spending one week in military jail for going AWOL to participate in (and win) the Mr Junior Europe bodybuilding competition.

Roald Dahl One of the UK's most beloved authors achieved the rank of wing commander in the RAF and even spent time working for MI6.

Mr T Before the gold-chain-donning and steadfast refusal to travel anywhere by plane, Mr T was a squad leader in the US Military Police Corps. While serving he was punished after being given the order by his sergeant to chop down trees as a training exercise. The sergeant neglected to tell him how many trees to tackle and Mr T single-handedly chopped down over 70 in the space of just three hours.

> " ... there are those who straight-up smack you in the face with shock to find out they ever served. "

Clint Eastwood The double Oscar-winner was drafted into the US Military during the Korean War, where he survived the crashing of the Douglas bomber he was flying in.

Sir Ian Fleming The creator of 007 (and not forgetting *Chitty Chitty Bang Bang*) was a commander in the Royal Navy. His code name was the slightly less sexy 17F.

Steve McQueen One of the world's greatest actors and effortlessly cool blokes was also, apparently, hard as nails, spending three years in the US Marines as a tank driver.

Bear Grylls TV presenter and adventurer joined the Indian Army after leaving school before spending three years in the SAS, where he suffered a parachuting accident when his main canopy tore and split at 16,000 feet – plunging him to the ground. He underwent one year's rehabilitation at the military hospital at Headley Court before discharging himself and going off to climb Mount Everest.

FIELD MARSHAL MONTGOMERY'S RICE PUDDING

Field Marshal Bernard Law 'Monty' Montgomery was a British Army officer throughout both World Wars. However, it was during World War II that his legendary status was cemented. He commanded the Eighth Army in desert battles against his fiercest rival – Erwin 'Desert Fox' Rommel, which included the Battle of El Alamein, a major turning point in the war. He subsequently commanded in Sicily and Italy, before being given responsibility for planning the entire D-Day landings. On 4 May 1945 he took the German surrender at Lüneburg Heath in northern Germany, and after the war he became Chief of the Imperial General Staff.

> **"** … only drinks water, has to have the nine o'clock news and be in bed by ten, washes his own shirts, rice pudding his favourite food. **"**

While the man affectionately known as 'Monty' was undoubtedly an all-time British hero, he wasn't someone you would have wanted to go for a night out with. For one thing he didn't drink. Ever. Which for a member of the Armed Forces is practically sacrilegious. At his first lunch with 'Monty', Winston Churchill offered him a drink – alcohol, naturally – to which Monty replied, 'I neither drink nor smoke and am 100 per cent fit,' to which Churchill replied, 'Well I drink *and* smoke, and am 200 per cent fit.' One-nil to Winny. (As an aside, it's ironic that such a firm tee-totaller would also have a very boozy tipple named after him: the infamous Harry's Bar in Venice – where both the beloved-of-bridesmaids, Bellini, and James Bond's favourite snifter, the dry Martini were invented – is also the home of the Montgomery Martini. Celebrated novelist Ernest Hemingway was the first to order one and it is made up of 15 parts gin to 1 part dry vermouth because 'Monty' was said to like a ratio of 15 British soldiers to every 1 Nazi on the battlefield. It sounds potent and, no doubt, after a few Monty Martinis you'd happily take on the SS and Luftwaffe single-handed.)

The second reason for not going on a night out with Monty was he wasn't exactly a big fan of fun. Nancy Mitford, a famous novelist and *Sunday Times* journalist from the 1950s and 60s, tells in her book, *The Letters of Nancy Mitford*

(Sceptre, 1994), of the time she broke bread with the great man: 'I had my luncheon with Monty. He is terribly like my dad – watch in hand when I arrived (the first, luckily), only drinks water, has to have the nine o'clock news and be in bed by ten, washes his own shirts, rice pudding his favourite food. All my books by his bed and, when he gets to a daring passage, he washes it down with Deuteronomy.' (For the record, Deuteronomy is a part of the Old Testament that, among other things, stresses the worship of God above everything else and the death penalty for anyone who disobeys their parents, is extravagant with their cash or gets drunk.) So here is a man who doesn't drink, is in bed by ten, feels guilty about reading the dirty bits of books and thinks blowing a bit of cash should equal death – hardly Russell Brand, is he? But then Russell didn't win the war in Africa for us and that's why Monty's favourite dish – rice pudding – is in here and Brand's isn't.

For four servings

You will need:
40g butter
100g pudding rice
75g caster sugar
1 litre milk (full-fat is best)
150ml double cream
1 teaspoon vanilla extract or
    1 vanilla pod
salt (literally a pinch)
nutmeg for grating (or alternatively
    a good pinch of ground nutmeg)
big blobs of strawberry jam

How you do it:

1   Preheat the oven to 150°C/gas 2.
Melt the butter in a flameproof casserole
on the hob (you can use any dish that
you can both cook on the hob with and
then bung in the oven; alternatively, start
cooking it in a saucepan, then tip it into
an ovenproof dish before baking). When
the butter has melted, add the rice and
give it a quick stir to coat each grain in
the silky, creamy goodness.

2   Next, pour in your sugar, a little at
a time, and stir it until it is all dissolved.
(This is why you use caster sugar as
opposed to normal 'pop it in your tea'
sugar. Caster is much finer and so
dissolves much more quickly. You can use
the other sugar but be prepared to give
your arms a bit more of a workout while
you attempt to dissolve it all.) As you stir
you will see that the rice starts to swell as
it takes on all that lovely flavour. When
it does that, slowly pour in the milk and
keep stirring so that you end up with a
nice smooth mixture.

3   Now to your dish. Stir in the cream
and vanilla – if you are using a vanilla
pod, lay it flat, cut it in half and then
gently scrape a knife blade down the
length of it and add all the lovely tiny
black seeds into your pudding (keep the
pod to flavour another dish). Give it yet
another mix and add the salt, then turn
the heat up a little to bring the pud to a
gentle blipping simmer. At this point grate
a little nutmeg all over the surface (or
sprinkle on a good pinch of the ground

stuff) and then take it off the heat and
stick it into the oven to bake for 1½
hours. Keep an eye on it as it cooks, and
once the surface is a nice golden brown,
pop a lid on the pot (or cover it with
foil) to stop the top browning any further.
You'll know when it is ready when the
pudding gently wobbles like the belly of
Chunk from *The Goonies* doing the Truffle
Shuffle. Serve it up with a great big blob
of strawberry jam on top – or swirled
through if you are feeling artistic.

GET OUT OF JAIL FREE

There have been many (presumably made-up) stories over the years about prisoners escaping from jail cells by using a file hidden in a cake. But while it sounds just as ludicrous, in WWII some of our plucky chaps did actually escape POW camps with the aid of a Monopoly set...

As the war wore on, more and more of our bravest and best were being detained at the pleasure of the Third Reich, and so the MOD were constantly thinking of ways to break them out. This brilliantly bonkers plan began when trying to come up with a solution to an age-old conundrum: the first thing any potential escapee needed was an accurate map of their surroundings. The problem with common-or-garden paper maps was that they made a lot of noise when opened (especially in tricky, trying-not-to-get-captured situations) and, furthermore, if they got wet they were ruined. Some bright spark,

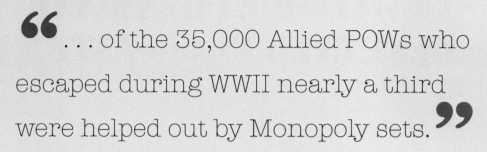

> " ... of the 35,000 Allied POWs who escaped during WWII nearly a third were helped out by Monopoly sets. "

therefore, came up with the idea of printing maps on silk as, not only were they silent when opened, they could be scrunched up into tiny balls to be hidden and were incredibly durable. Now it just so happened that there was only one manufacturer in the whole of Blighty who had perfected printing on silk and that was John Waddington Ltd – the chaps who make Monopoly. And it just so further happened that board games, like Monopoly, were accepted as part of care packages distributed by the Red Cross to prisoners of war. Putting two and two together, the MOD and the chaps at Waddingtons got to work and soon 'special' versions of the board game were

finding their way into the hands of men locked up in deepest, darkest Germany. Not only did the boards contain the silk maps (hidden in tiny carved depressions in the board that were covered over by the finished playing surface) but also a small compass, real German, Italian and French currency hidden among the Monopoly money and, finally, in honour of the cake that started this story, a metal file.

The board games immediately proved successful and while exact figures are unknown, rumours abound that of the 35,000 Allied POWs who escaped during WWII nearly a third were helped out by Monopoly sets.

SIR RANULPH FIENNES'S VANILLA ICE CREAM AND BEST EVER CHOCOLATE SAUCE

Sir Ranulph Twisleton-Wykeham-Fiennes OBE, is a British adventurer, award winning author, and the man *The Guinness Book of World Records* once described as the world's greatest living explorer. Fiennes served in the British Army for eight years, beginning his career in the Royal Scots Greys in their tank division. In the 1960s he was recruited into the SAS and, once there, he was soon promoted and became the youngest-ever captain in the British Army. After leaving the Services he began his series of record-breaking 'firsts', including being the first person to visit both North and South Poles, the first man to cross both the Antarctic and Arctic Oceans, and the first man to circumnavigate the world along its polar axis – a feat that has never been repeated. Sir Ranulph, just one year shy of his seventieth birthday, attempted to take on one of the last-remaining polar challenges – to cross Antarctica in winter – in an adventure the media called 'The Coldest Journey on Earth', but he had to pull out of the expedition when he suffered frostbite.

It's a point we have returned to time and again but one of the most important roles food plays to a serving man or woman is that of comfort. That chocolate biscuit is a brief respite from a terrible situation that we civvies would struggle to cope with. This central tenet even holds true for a living legend such as Sir Ranulph Fiennes. This is a man who, at the age of sixty-five, climbed to the summit of Mount Everest and who, back in 2003, only three months after a massive heart attack, a three-day coma and a double heart bypass, achieved the first ever 'seven by seven by seven' – seven marathons in seven consecutive days on all seven continents.

> ❝ . . . we all need a bit of TLC from time to time and this recipe will deliver bowls full of it. ❞

Tough as old boots – yet what meal does he recommend for our delectation? Ice cream topped off with his 'best ever' chocolate sauce. Comfort food if ever we heard it. Sir Ranulph tells us the recipe came from his late wife, Ginny, and it was something that they both enjoyed enormously, as well as being something he himself turned to when spirits were low during his time serving in the Forces. It doesn't matter how hard you are, we all need a bit of TLC from time to time and this recipe will deliver bowls full of it.

For two servings

You will need:

150ml milk
1 tablespoon instant coffee
  granules
1 Mars bar (or similar chocolate
  bar)
vanilla ice cream

How you do it:

1 Start by taking a small saucepan and popping it on a low heat on the hob – go for a low and slow start because you'll next be adding the milk and you don't want it to boil and spoil. Okay, so now add the milk and, as it slowly heats up, chop up the chocolate bar into nice, thin slices. (If they were big and thick this melting process would take forever.)

2 Before the milk starts to boil (if it looks like it is going to, simply lift the pan off the hob for a minute or two to reduce the heat back down), add the coffee granules and stir until they have dissolved. Then add in the sliced chocolate and stir gently until it's melted and blended into the milk, then let it simmer a minute or two more until thick and rich.

3 While it's ticking away in the pan, scoop out two generous helpings of vanilla ice cream (the best you can get your hands on) and then pour the chocolate sauce all over and immediately attack with a spoon.

ANDY MCNAB'S LAMB TAGINE

Andy McNab joined the Army in 1976 before making the move to 22 SAS Regiment in 1984. During his ten years with the SAS he worked on both covert and overt special operations worldwide, including anti-terrorist and anti-drug operations in the Middle and Far East, South and Central America and Northern Ireland. In the First Gulf War, McNab commanded the famous Bravo Two Zero patrol – an eight-man team tasked with destroying underground communication links in Iraq and with finding and destroying Scud missile launchers. One of four men taken prisoner, McNab was held for six weeks and was savagely tortured. McNab was the British Army's most highly decorated serving soldier when he finally left the SAS in February 1993. McNab has since written a number of bestselling books, both fiction and non-fiction, worked as a technical weapons adviser on Hollywood films and is a director of a security company that trains civilians who work in hostile environments.

As mentioned in the last chapter, this is one of two recipes that Andy was kind enough to donate to us, but this is definitely the one you're more likely to have heard of/eaten/seen on a menu in a restaurant (see page 112 for the 'other one'!). While it may sound fancy, it is, basically, a spicy lamb stew – a good, hearty dish made for men who are measured by square footage. It gets its name from the special earthenware pot that it is cooked in – the 'tagine' (though don't worry, you don't need to rush out and buy a new bit of kit to cook this recipe: a casserole will do just as well; if you do want to get one, however, it should set you back no more than about £20). The dish is cooked all across North Africa and especially in Morocco and Tunisia, which is presumably where Andy was when he first came across it. Over to the man himself:

'I bought a traditional clay tagine pot on my travels at some point, and decided this made me a good cook. Can't say I am still regularly cooking with it, but I am a big fan of lamb tagine.'

And after trying this dish once, we're sure you will be too.

For four servings

You will need:
splash of olive oil
800g lamb shoulder
1 large onion
1 fresh red chilli, deseeded and finely chopped
2 garlic cloves
1 teaspoon ground cinnamon
1 teaspoon ground cumin
1 teaspoon ground ginger
1 teaspoon ground turmeric
1 teaspoon paprika
450ml lamb, chicken or vegetable stock (fresh or made up from a stock cube)
400g can of chopped tomatoes
400g dried apricots, roughly chopped
400g couscous
salt and pepper
a little chopped fresh parsley
a little chopped fresh mint
a few flaked almonds

How you do it:

1 If you're planning on going fully native then start by heating the olive oil in a flameproof tagine, but as we said, fear not if you don't have one – you can just use a casserole. (However, whatever you do choose to cook in, it has to be something that you can both fry ingredients in on the hob and transfer into a hot oven.)

2 While the oil is heating up, cut the lamb into cubes and then fry them. What's good about this dish is that you can use a relatively cheap cut of lamb – the shoulder for example – as the meat is going to be slow-cooked for a while and so the tougher (and cheaper) bits work very well for this. No point using prime lamb steaks here. Okay, once the cubes have fried for about 5 minutes or so (or until they are browned all over), take them out of the pot with a slotted spoon and set them to one side.

3 Next, peel and chop the onion and fry it, stirring, in all that lovely meat juice, again for just 5 minutes.

4 To the fried onion, now add the chopped red chilli, the garlic and all other

spices, and cook for a further minute or two before popping the lamb back in and giving it a good mix through. Once that's done, add the stock and give it a good stir. Finally, for now, chuck in the contents of the can of chopped tomatoes, the dried apricots and as much salt and pepper as you feel it needs.

5 Now you have a choice: pop on the lid, get the whole lot boiling and then turn the heat down so it simmers on the hob for 1–1½ hours until really tender; or transfer it it into a hot oven (200°C/ gas 6) for the same amount of time. Either way, check it occasionally to make sure the lamb has gone nice and flaky

and tender and the sauce has thickened, adding a little water or leftover stock if it starts to dry out.

6 When the tagine is good and ready, make the couscous. This couldn't be easier as it basically entails measuring out however much couscous the packet says for four people and pouring over the right amount of boiling water or stock and a pinch of salt, and, er, that's it. It sits for a few minutes while it soaks up the water before you fluff it up with a fork and serve. Then plate up a generous dollop of tagine with a scoop of couscous and a little parsley, mint and almonds sprinkled over the top to garnish.

MICHAEL MORPURGO'S CHICKEN ROGAN JOSH WITH RICE AND PAPADUMS

Michael Morpurgo OBE is an English author, poet, playwright and former Children's Laureate who is best known for his award-winning book *War Horse*, which has been both a hugely successful stage play and, more recently, an Oscar-nominated Steven Spielberg film. Michael trained to be an officer for the British Army at the Royal Military Academy at Sandhurst.

While Michael's time in the Forces was short, he still professes very fond memories of training to be an officer and the excellent curries he was served at Sandhurst: 'One dish that immediately springs to mind is a spicy chicken curry we regularly had, that came with mountains of rice and papadums.'

Beyond his brief period marching, shooting and shouting (that's what trainee officers do, right?), Michael's greater contribution to the British Forces was in writing his famous book. The novel brings to light both the horrific conditions and the exceptional human and animal sacrifices that were made during the Great War. Inspired by meeting WWI veterans who had each served alongside horses, Michael's compelling story delivers the shocking news that some 10 million horses died during the conflict and, of the 1 million that were given no choice but to fight and serve in the British Army, a mere 62,000 made it back alive. Couple this with the devastating loss of human life – 2 per cent of the entire population of the UK died during the War – and Michael helps us to see what a dark time this was and, by doing so, hopefully, ensures such a thing does not happen again.

Back to the food, and what we've selected in Michael's honour is a rogan josh – traditionally made with lamb but can be done just as well with chicken. We've chosen rogan josh because, with its high number of ingredients and degree of complexity, it's something that's been the sole preserve of officers from as far back as the days of the Raj. Meanwhile, across camp, squaddies tend to get something a bit more basic for their curry. In fact, many within the Forces claim that nothing shows the difference between privates and officers more than the curry they are served . . . and this one is, undoubtedly, fit for royalty.

Please don't be put off by the longer-than-normal list of ingredients here, as once you have them all assembled, this really is quite a straightforward recipe. And, better than that, you get to cook with lager, so can (for once) legitimately justify the cans lined up on the kitchen work surface.

For four servings

You will need:

2 garlic cloves

2 onions

1 thumb-sized piece of fresh ginger

1 teaspoon ground turmeric

1 teaspoon chilli powder (more if you like it ultra-hot)

1 teaspoon garam masala

1 teaspoon ground cinnamon

2 teaspoons ground cumin

2 teaspoons ground coriander

2 tablespoons tomato purée

salt and pepper

vegetable or sunflower oil

50–60g butter

800g diced chicken meat

300ml chicken stock (fresh or made with a stock cube)

400g can of chopped tomatoes

100ml plain yoghurt

300ml lager

400g basmati rice

chopped fresh coriander for garnish (optional)

For the papadums:

250g plain flour

¼ teaspoon ground black pepper

¼ teaspoon salt

¼ teaspoon ground cumin

3–4 tablespoons water

How you do it:

1 We're going to start by making our own curry paste and to do this you'll ideally be in possession of a food processor or blender to save yourself not only a lot of time but also a lot of potential blood-letting what with all the fine chopping, bashing and slicing you will have to do otherwise. Peel the garlic, onions and ginger and bung them into the blender along with all the spices (turmeric, chilli powder, garam masala, ground cinnamon, ground cumin, ground coriander), the tomato purée and a good pinch of salt and pepper, and blitz the lot to within an inch of its life. What you're left with is a lovely, flavour-packed curry paste to cook the chicken in. If the paste looks a little dry, then glug in a teaspoon or two of olive oil and whizz it again. (If you are going the Luddite route and not using a blender, then you'll need to chop the ginger, onion and garlic as finely as you can before giving them, and the rest of the ingredients, a damn good thrashing in a bowl with the end of a rolling pin or, if you have the wherewithal, use a pestle and mortar.)

2   Next, put a splash of oil into a frying pan, add the butter, and get the lot going over a medium heat. Add the diced chicken with a pinch of salt and pepper, and brown on all sides. Next, add the curry paste and make sure the chicken is coated in it before frying and stirring for a further 5 minutes.

3   Next, add the chicken stock, can of tomatoes, yoghurt and, of course, the lager and mix it all together well. Turn up the heat until the sauce begins to boil and then cover with a lid, turn the heat right down low and let it simmer very gently for 1 hour. Lift the lid every so often and give it a stir and make sure it

isn't drying out – if it looks in danger of doing so, add in a splash of water and stir again.

4   While the curry is merrily cooking away, crack on with the papadums, and the rice. Start with the papadums as they take a bit more work. Pop the flour in a large bowl (not for the quantity of ingredients but because you will need to get your mitts in there in a minute) with the pepper, salt and cumin and give them a good mix. Slowly add the water and then get your hands in and start kneading it all together to form a dough. When it's a plasticine-like consistency (if it's too wet add in a little more flour, too stiff add a little more water), take out a golf-ball-sized piece and dump it onto a floured work surface (the flour will help ensure the dough doesn't stick). Then flatten it with your hand and roll it as thin as possible with a rolling pin. When it is papadum-thin, cut it into a circle. If your eye isn't true, or your hand steady, you can always cut around a small plate. Repeat this process until you have as many papadums as you can make from the dough.

5   In a deep pan (because you don't want hot oil splashing everywhere), add about 500ml of vegetable or sunflower oil and heat on full blast. When the oil is very hot, gently lower in a papadum and cook for a minute or so, before carefully turning over and frying for another minute on the other side until crisp and puffy. Take out with tongs and drain on kitchen paper. Repeat for each lovely disc.

6   Finally, cook the rice. Bring a pan of salted water to the boil. Tip in the rice, stir, bring back to the boil and cook, giving it the occasional stir, until it is done. As this will only take 10–15 minutes, it's best to leave it until the curry has been going for 45 minutes, so that the two of them are ready at roughly the same time.

7   When the rice is done, drain it in a colander, then pop the colander back over the saucepan. When all is ready, spoon the rice onto plates, add a good dollop of rogan josh topped off with some chopped coriander along with a tottering tower of crispy papadums.

CHRISTMAS IN THE FORCES

As we all know from The Farm's 'All Together Now' and Paul 'Macca' McCartney's 'Pipes of Peace', Christmas on the front line hasn't been much fun. Outside of the occasional impromptu kickabout, it was pretty much business as usual in the shooting and killing stakes.

While they won't find themselves in a boggy no-man's-land scrapping with Germans, it's not really much different for our modern-day troops when it comes to the morale-sapping fact of being away from home for the festive season. One thing that can make a huge difference, though, is food, and what all our bases across the globe aim to do is serve every soldier who wants one a roast turkey dinner with as many of the classic trimmings as they can muster. Even those in the field on The Day are able to indulge in a bit of festive spirit – special Christmas dinner ration packs are prepared and many also have foodie gifts from home to bring them some comfort. A mini Christmas pud or a little jar of brandy butter can be a real boost when camped out in the middle of nowhere.

So, next 25 December, spare a thought for the brave boys and girls doing their bit far away from home and their loved ones. They'd swap places with you in an instant.

CHRIS RYAN'S SPICY CHICKEN AND RICE

Chris Ryan joined the SAS in 1984 and, during his ten years with the regiment, was involved in various overt and covert operations including being sniper commander of the anti-terrorist team. During the First Gulf War, Chris was the only member of the Bravo Two Zero eight-man patrol to escape from Iraq. Of the rest, three colleagues were killed and four captured (Andy McNab being one of them, if you recall, see page 130). It was the longest escape and evasion in the history of the SAS. For this he was awarded the Military Medal. During Ryan's last two years in the regiment he selected and trained potential SAS recruits. He left the Forces in 1994 and works now as a security expert as well as appearing on a number of TV shows.

Just proving that real men cook, hard-as-nails SAS veteran Chris Ryan has kindly donated this recipe – Spicy Chicken and Rice – which was his favourite from his time in the Forces. This dish comes from his mother-in-law and Chris recalls making it on many occasions, having particularly fond memories of cooking it both near (while on the anti-terrorist team when he was fortunate enough to get home most nights) and far (when trekking through the jungles of Brunei, Belize and Indonesia). While out on these expeditions, he and his team had to survive on basic rations, but once a week they would get a 'fresh day' when meat and vegetables came in, and that's when he would break out this bad boy. (Showing a further commitment to cooking a decent meal that we should all salute him for, he carried the spices he needed in waterproof containers.) So enjoy this recipe – it's a cracker and, let's be honest, the closest most of us will get to being in the SAS.

For four servings

You will need:

- 4 skinless chicken breasts
- 1 teaspoon ground cumin
- 1 teaspoon ground coriander
- 1 teaspoon cayenne pepper
- 1 teaspoon sweet paprika
- pinch of chilli powder (optional)
- 1 tablespoon plain flour
- 400g basmati or other long-grain rice
- large knob of butter
- splash of olive oil
- 1 scotch bonnet chilli pepper, deseeded and chopped
- 2 onions, chopped
- 250ml boiling water
- 1 chicken stock cube
- 2 teaspoons tomato chutney (preferably Baxters, Chris's preferred brand)
- 2 teaspoons soft brown sugar
- 1 ziplock plastic bag

How you do it:

1   Start with the meat. Dice the chicken breasts into rough 2.5cm cubes (you don't have to get the ruler out, just cut into bite-sized chunks) and then put the meat into a ziplock plastic bag. Add to the bag the cumin, coriander, cayenne pepper, paprika and – if you like it ultra-spicy – chilli powder (but don't forget you will be adding in a scotch bonnet later, so don't overdo it!). Finally, add the flour before sealing up the bag and giving the chicken a good old rub in the spicy mix. (Dry-rubbing the meat is a popular cooking technique for many recipes. It's particularly good for prepping meat for BBQs – and a great way to get loads of flavour into your chosen dish.) Set it aside for a few minutes to get good and coated.

2   Bring a pan of salted water to the boil, then chuck in the rice, stir and leave it to for 10 minutes or according to the packet directions. Drain in a colander, then cover with a lid or tin foil and keep warm until ready to serve.

3   While the rice is cooking, heat the butter and olive oil in a saucepan. Add the spiced chicken and fry – keeping it moving all the time to ensure it doesn't burn or catch and cooks evenly on all sides. As the chicken is cooking, add in your chopped scotch bonnet chilli. Now be warned, this is a hot, hot chilli (what else would the SAS eat?!) so if you don't like your dishes too spicy perhaps think about replacing it with a milder one like a jalapeño.

4   When the chicken is browned all over, add the chopped onion, and continue frying for a few minutes. When the onion is browned nicely, add the boiling water and crumble in the chicken stock cube. Stir well, then let the whole lot simmer so that a nice, thick sauce starts to take shape: 5–10 minutes should do it, but keep an eye on it until it is a consistency you like, (if it thickens too much, you can, of course, add a little more water). When the sauce is just right, add the tomato chutney and brown sugar. Give the whole lot a good mix through and simmer away for a further 10–15 minutes, again adding a little boiling water if becoming too dry. Serve a hearty portion of the spicy chicken on a portion of rice and get stuck in.

PRINCE HARRY'S BANGERS AND MASH

Captain Henry Charles Albert David Windsor of the Blues and Royals Army Air Corps began his military career in 2005 when he enrolled in the Royal Military Academy at Sandhurst. Within a year he had completed his officer training and became a cornet in the Blues and Royals, before being promoted to lieutenant just two years later. During this time he became the first royal to see active service in over

thirty years when he was deployed as a forward air controller in the Helmand Province of Afghanistan. Prince Harry has since undergone three years of Apache helicopter training and has been promoted to the rank of captain. He returned to active service in January 2013 with a stint in Afghanistan.

Now we need to make one thing very clear from the start as we don't want to end up in the Tower, nor do we want to minimise our chances of one day being knighted, so it's only appropriate to declare that this recipe hasn't been 'donated' by Prince Harry in the same way the others in this chapter have. We asked the royal household for the prince's favourite dish but, sadly, they couldn't help. Well, we're not one to take 'no' for an answer and so, showing that indomitable British bulldog spirit that won us famous victories at Agincourt, Dunkirk and last place at the Eurovision Song Contest, we ploughed ahead anyway. Hunting high and low we subsequently found an interview Prince Harry gave in 2008 while out in Afghanistan. Serving

in Helmand Province, the prince, like the rest of the serving men, had to live off the twenty-four-hour ration packs, detailed in Chapter 2. While the food at bases like Camp Bastion can be great – cracking roasts, curries and the like – surviving on those ration packs day after day, week after week, can be a bit, well, dispiriting. 'Rations are miserable,' Prince Harry said. 'I've been on them for I can't remember how long. The guys here have been on them for even longer. They really are fed up with it, but food's food.' When asked what meal he was craving, he immediately came up with a British classic: 'Bangers and mash with gravy would be brilliant – awesome.' Harry also rightly suggested that this would be something all serving troops would enjoy and even wondered if Jamie Oliver would do for army rations what he did for school dinners. Sadly Mr O hasn't yet been able to help, allowing us to sweep in and take the glory (and, perhaps, an MBE – just a suggestion, Ma'am) as we give you this recipe for tiptop sausage and mash.

> **"When asked what meal he was craving, he immediately came up with a British classic: 'Bangers and mash with gravy would be brilliant – awesome'."**

However, a word about the ingredients before we start, as you'll want to pick the best sausages and potatoes for the dish. When it comes to bangers, the truth of the matter is 'you get what you pay for'. A cheap, smooth-textured, bright pink banger will almost certainly have the lowest percentage of meat they can get away with and will contain more filler, such as rusk and the bits of animal they force people to eat on *I'm a Celebrity ... Get Me Out of Here*. However, we don't want you to think you *have* to spend a fortune and find a 100 per cent pure meat banger. An all-meat sausage can be quite chewy to tackle, so you may prefer a bit of fat and breadcrumbs in there to keep your banger soft, moist and tasty. In terms of cost, your best bet is to go to your local butcher and ask him to give you the best four snags for the cash in your pocket. Usually hand-made on the premises, they will taste infinitely better than a shrink-wrapped set from the supermarket.

You can use any variety of spud but, as you are aiming for the perfect mash, you need to find ones with a fairly floury texture rather than waxy ones. The reason being that floury spuds will start to break up when they have been boiled, whereas waxy ones tend to retain their shape even if you've been boiling away for ages. Good all-round spuds are Maris Piper or Desirée, or you could go with King Edward or Rooster, which are further up the floury spectrum.

For one serving

You will need:
- 4 sausages (the best you can afford)
- 1 large potato
- salt and pepper
- knob of butter
- 2 tablespoons single or double cream
- 1 tablespoon milk, if necessary
- gravy granules
- 1 onion (optional)

How you do it:

1 Before you attack the sausages, it's time to tackle a myth – that you need to prick them before cooking. The reason people say this is that, back in the days of rationing, bangers were bulked out with a lot of water and fat so when heated to the right levels had an annoying tendency to explode, showering all and sundry in molten pig bits. Nowadays, though, even the cheapest snag isn't likely to blow up, so not only is pricking it unnecessary, it actually means the moisture, fat and juices seep out of your sausage and make it much less tasty. So instead of puncturing your bangers, bung them in a foil-lined baking tin, lightly brushed with a little oil if you're using 100 per cent meat ones, and pop them in a preheated oven at 180°C/gas 4 for about 20 minutes, turning them over at the halfway mark for the perfect results. Easy.

2 While the bangers are cooking, tackle the mash. Once you've chosen your potatoes, peel and chop them until they are roughly golf-ball-sized and pop them in a pan with just enough water to cover them (straight out of a boiling kettle if you want to speed everything up).

Chuck in a good pinch of salt and whack up the heat to get them boiling. When they are bubbling away, cover with a lid, reduce the heat and simmer for 15–20 minutes or so, but be sure to test every 5 minutes to see if they are done – if the fork goes in easily they are ready to go. Drain in a colander and then pop them back into the pan to dry out briefly before adding the butter, and cream a little at a time. Mash with a masher (or ricer if you want it super-smooth) and stop when you get to a consistency you like, adding a splash of milk if necessary. Mix through a little salt and pepper until you are happy with the taste.

3 Finally, mix up your gravy according to the jar's instructions (usually adding boiling water to a measure of granules and stirring like mad; life is too short to make your own gravy from scratch, but, to be really flash, you could fry some sliced onions until golden brown and stir them in to make a delicious onion gravy), and serve the lot with a good dollop of English mustard. A meal fit for a king or, in this instance, for his kid brother.

> ❝ Rations are miserable . . . I've been on them for I can't remember how long. ❞

LAWRENCE OF ARABIA'S DEAD CAMEL AND OTHER FUN FACTS

Whether it be to show off down the pub, win at Trivial Pursuit or just to pass an idle moment, everyone enjoys a fun fact or two. Here, then, are a few Forces ones for your delectation:

• At the British Army's main base in Afghanistan – Camp Bastion in Helmand Province – the chefs get through a staggering 7,500 burgers, 2.5 tons of chicken breasts, 20,000 baguettes and 4.5 tons of chips a week.

• A permanent British Army didn't come into existence until 1661. Before this point, a fighting force was raised only when war broke out. Many in the country were uneasy with the idea of a 'standing' army and so a special bill was passed to say that it could only exist in peacetime with the say-so of parliament. This permission is still required today and so every year a new bill is passed.

• The last battle to be fought on British soil was the Battle of Culloden in 1746.

• Yorkie chocolate bars have always been aimed at men but did you know that they do a special version of the bar just for the British Forces? The Yorkie chocolate bar found on British military bases tastes the same but in place of its usual 'It's not for girls!' slogan has, instead, 'It's not for civvies!'

• Left and right boots were not introduced into the Army until 1843. Before then boots were the same for both feet.

• Shrapnel was invented by a Brit, Henry Shrapnel, of the Royal Artillery. It was first used in 1804.

• Macédoine is regularly served to our British boys and girls but what the heck is it? Well it's small, diced mixed veg – they get it in cans – that can be eaten hot or cold.

• The Royal Tank Corps sports a nifty black beret as its regimental headgear, the idea coming after some World War I RTC officers admired the French wearing their traditional berets. However, it wasn't 'the done thing' to copy the French (of course) and so the corps instead contacted a load of English girls' boarding schools to ask for samples of the ones they wore.

• The great British military man and acclaimed film subject Lawrence of Arabia accidentally shot his own camel in the back of the head during a charge against the Turkish Army.

JOSH LEWSEY'S FULL ENGLISH BREAKFAST

Owen Joshua Lewsey MBE is a former England rugby union player. He joined London Wasps at eighteen, won his first England cap in 1998 and went on to play for his country on a further fifty-five occasions. He won every major trophy in both the domestic and international game including a World Cup victory in 2003. Josh also attended the Royal Military Academy at Sandhurst, where he graduated in 2001 before serving two years as an officer in the British Army with the Royal Artillery. He retired from the sport in 2009 and now works in the City.

When it comes to officers in the British Army, we are fortunate to be able to count among their number men like Lewsey. If you're being expected to attack an enemy line armed with nothing more than a can opener and a wry sense of humour, it helps to have a man-mountain like Lewsey to lead you on: someone who not only survived the hardcore training at Sandhurst but also excelled in one of the world's toughest sports. To go to Australia for the World Cup of 2003 and beat the home team in their own back yard takes true front-line grit. This physical and mental toughness was clearly honed during his time in the Army, as Josh recalls:

'Any member of the British Army will be more than familiar with the notion of the wetlands – a.k.a. the Brecon Beacons (a favourite army training location) – which, for some reason, seems to attract its own terrible micro-climate. The Sandhurst intake of 2001 "fortuitously" timed its manoeuvres there, with not only the foot-

> **"** . . . if the Archangel Gabriel himself had descended at that very moment, he would not have significantly improved the exultation, joy and delight that that breakfast provided. **"**

and-mouth crisis, but also the wettest year on record. Fast-forward to the legendary Crooken's Challenge: torrential rain, an ambush that never arrived (which, essentially, meant my platoon and I lying in a puddle all night for nothing) and a directing staff who believed "there is never any need for warm kit on these isles". Basically, [it is] the greatest valley of morale-sapping darkness, misery, depression and despair known to man. However, cue first light – a break in the clouds, morning sunshine and breakfast: 10 minutes without shouting, a warm sweet brew and a piping hot boil-in-the-bag breakfast of sausage and beans. Hark – tears, smiles and happiness! Quite honestly, if the Archangel Gabriel himself had descended at that very moment, he would not have significantly improved the exultation, joy and delight that that breakfast provided.'

Josh's recollection not only gives us immense pride and humility in the extreme efforts the Forces go through on our behalf (and makes us simultaneously glad we don't have to), but also goes

to show – on the food front – that sometimes it's the simple dishes that give the most pleasure. With Josh's permission we're going to expand a wee bit beyond a simple recipe for boil-in-the-bag sausage and beans (which would simply mean heating the pack up and eating) and, instead, show you how to make the perfect Full English. Something we can be just as proud of as we are of men and officers like Josh.

Like deciding on the best Bond girl/cure for a hangover/way to suitably punish whoever came up with the 'Go Compare' opera singer, everyone has an opinion when it comes to the Full English. Some can't stand the sight of black pudding, some want scrambled eggs instead of fried and some, truly weird people, don't like bacon. So in calling this the 'perfect' Full English, we realise there will be plenty out there who disagree. All we can do is show you how to cook each of the ingredients in the simplest and best way possible and, like a man who owns his own tailor, you can suit yourself.

For one serving

You will need:

- 2 sausages (the best quality you can afford)
- a little vegetable, sunflower or olive oil
- 2–3 rashers of bacon
- 1 thick slice of black pudding
- 1 large mushroom
- 2 vine tomatoes (if you can get them – normal tomatoes if you can't)
- 1 slice of white bread
- 2 large free-range eggs
- ½ x 400g can of Heinz baked beans
- tomato ketchup, brown sauce and steaming hot tea, to serve

How you do it:

1 Start with the sausages, as they take the longest to cook. The simplest way to ensure a perfect banger is to pop in a foil-lined baking tin (lightly oiled if all-meat sausages) in a preheated oven at 180°C/gas 4 for 20 minutes (turning them over halfway through). That way the sausages will come out cooked through but still juicy and nice and brown on the outside. (By the way, if you muck up your timings with any of the ingredients and have some ready before others, don't panic, just simply pop the finished item on a plate sitting on the lowest shelf of the oven – the coolest part – turned down as low as it will go and it will keep it warm until you are ready to plate up.)

2 On to the bacon, and there are a couple of options: either pop them under the grill for a couple of minutes per side (a little longer if you prefer it crispy) or fry them in a little oil in a pan – again 2 minutes or so per side. Grilling is healthier as the fat drips away but the bacon is, arguably, tastier in the pan because the fat sticks around. It's your call.

3 Black pudding is not to everyone's taste so feel free to omit it if you don't like the idea of eating congealed pig's blood, but for those who like the earthy taste, stick under the grill for 1½–2 minutes each side until crispy (you can, of course, do this at the same time as the bacon, if cooking both).

4 Mushroom next: just wipe away any dirt (don't wash or the mushroom will absorb the water like a sponge), drizzle over a little oil and sprinkle over some salt and pepper, before frying in a hot pan for a couple of minutes per side.

5 For the tomatoes, we're suggesting vine tomatoes as they tend to have a more intense flavour (like normal tomatoes but with taste rating cranked up to eleven). But whichever you use, you want them heated through not overcooked as that will turn them to mush. Cut them in half, drizzle with oil before seasoning with salt and pepper and grilling for 2 minutes on both sides.

6 Fried bread is just that – a slice of bread gently fried in fat. As super-tasty

as it is unhealthy. Heat a frying pan over a medium heat and cover the base with oil – you need a fair dollop in there – before adding the bread and cooking for 2–3 minutes each side until crispy and golden. If you want to add a little butter to your oil, it will taste even better.

7   Now for the eggs. You can go one of three ways here. Fried eggs are the most traditional so we'll start there. For a more thorough breakdown of frying an egg look at Chapter 1's Egg Banjo, but the shorthand version is as follows: crack the egg straight into a pan set over a medium heat with some oil in it, leave it there until the egg white turns, erm, white and you are happy with how runny/cooked it is. Gently remove from the pan with a fish slice. Next up is poaching. There are many tricks of the trade but the easiest way to poach one (if you're not using any specialist equipment) is to boil some water and while it's heating up, crack the egg gently into the middle of a suitably sized

square of clingfilm. Carefully lift each corner of the clingfilm until the egg sits in the middle in a big teardrop shape. Tie the ends off in a knot and pop the egg

> ❝Sometimes it's the simple dishes that give the most pleasure.❞

into the boiling water for 2–3 minutes. Fish out after this time and carefully cut away the clingfilm to produce a perfect poached egg. Finally on the oeuf front there is scrambled. Again there are

plenty of ways to do this but the easiest is to use a microwave. Crack the eggs into a bowl and whisk them up with a little salt, pepper, a splash of milk and a knob of butter, then zap them in the microwave for 20 seconds at a time, mixing them through with a fork at the end of every session. You do it in short bursts because it's a bit hit and miss as to when they will be ready, and there is nothing worse than overcooked scrambled eggs. When the eggs look very nearly done – i.e. there is still a little runny egg in the bowl – stop and take out of the microwave. The eggs will continue to cook a little after they are removed from the oven, and become just set and creamy. Give them a final mix through.

8   Last but by no means least, open up a can of Heinz beans – and only Heinz – and heat through in a pan.

9   Once all the separate bits are cooked, serve up and enjoy with dollops of tomato ketchup and brown sauce and a mug of steaming hot tea. Perfection.

JOHNSON BEHARRY'S CHICKEN AND MUSHROOM INSTANT NOODLES

Lance Corporal Johnson Gideon Beharry of the 1st Battalion, Princess of Wales's Royal Regiment, is a British Army soldier who was awarded the Victoria Cross – the highest military decoration for valour in the British Armed Forces – for twice saving members of his unit from ambush while in Iraq. On 1 May 2004, Beharry was driving a Warrior armoured vehicle that was hit by multiple rocket-propelled grenades. The platoon commander, the vehicle's gunner and a number of other soldiers in the vehicle were injured. Due to damage, Beharry was forced to open his hatch to steer the vehicle, exposing his face and head to small-arms fire. Beharry drove the crippled vehicle through the ambush, leading his own crew and five other Warriors to safety. Back on duty on 11 June 2004, Beharry was again driving the lead Warrior of his platoon when it was ambushed. A rocket-propelled grenade hit the vehicle 15cm from his head, resulting in serious shrapnel injuries to his face and brain. Other rockets then hit the vehicle, incapacitating his commander and injuring several of the crew. Despite his life-threatening injuries, Beharry retained control of his vehicle and drove it out of the ambush area before losing consciousness. Beharry was formally invested with the Victoria Cross by the queen on 27 April 2005. Beharry is the first recipient of the VC since 1982, and the youngest ever, aged just twenty-six when he was honoured.

Read that last bit again. *Twenty-six years old.* From our experience, the biggest achievement of most guys of that age involves beating all-comers on FIFA, not committing two acts of incredible bravery while fighting for their country. Amazing.

You might, therefore, have expected us to be sharing a recipe for something fancy, something suitable for a man of such stature – a dish made of caviar, oysters or other highfalutin ingredients.

But just going to show he is not only mind-scramblingly brave but also exceptionally down-to-earth, Johnson told us his favourite Forces meal is the instant noodle dish so beloved of students (you know the ones we mean).

> **"**. . . boil kettle, open pack, pour water, stir, scoff.**"**

Now if we strictly followed that recipe this would be one of the shortest entries in the book – boil kettle, open pack, pour water, stir, scoff – so, in Johnson's honour, we're going to show you how to make a pimped-up version of the classic, pre-made variety – chicken and mushroom – that tastes much more awesome . . .

For one serving

You will need:

1 teaspoon cornflour
1 teaspoon curry powder
1 nest of dried egg noodles
50g cooked chicken breast
4 mushrooms
splash of olive oil (optional)
½ onion, roughly chopped
1 garlic clove, roughly chopped
splash of soy sauce
salt and pepper

How you do it:

1 To make our version of the popular student snack, you're going to need something to put it in, something you can take with you and fill up with boiling water at a later date – a jar (no, not a cheeky pint before we start, an actual jam jar). First thing you need to do is make sure it is thoroughly clean, so give it a wash through in the hottest, water you can stand with a squeeze of washing-up liquid. Then rinse it really well. When it's squeaky clean, put it

and the lid on a baking tray and pop the lot into an oven at 110°C/gas ¼. Don't be tempted to go any hotter than that as the glass can crack. Leave for 30 minutes and then bring them out and make sure they are bone dry before you fill them up. (If you want a simpler alternative, just use a sealable plastic lunch box that you have run through the dishwasher at its hottest setting. Again make sure it is dry before putting the ingredients in.)

2 Now on to the recipe. First mix the cornflour with the curry powder (any you fancy from fiery hot to mild) and drop it into the bottom of the clean container. (The cornflour is there to thicken your sauce when you add the water later on.) Next, pop in your nest of dry noodles. You can buy packets of dried noodles in most supermarkets and they only take three to four minutes to 'cook' when added to boiling water. You can also use pre-cooked noodles, which will heat through in the boiling water, but you will need to eat that snack much more quickly as they don't

keep as long as the dried variety. (And, come on, dried is more authentic if we are trying to make a grown-up version of the student classic. Though we don't recommend taking the whole authenticity

thing too far; we don't suggest you start paying for your round at the pub by cheque or waking up just in time for *Countdown* on the TV, for instance.)

3　Now for the chicken. You need the ready-cooked sort you use in sandwiches (or a bit left over from the Sunday roast) as you're just, basically, heating it through with the boiling water and not cooking it, and it goes without saying that salmonella is an unwelcome ingredient in any meal. We suggest using pieces of actual chicken breast as opposed to the sliced, pressed variety for a more meaty bite. Whichever you go for, chop it up in very small pieces and drop it in your container. Now for the mushrooms, and you can go a couple of ways here too. If you have time, slice them and then fry them up in a little oil before allowing them to cool and then dropping in your chosen container. Alternatively, you can use raw mushrooms just so long as they are very finely sliced, as if they are thin enough, the boiling water will be enough to heat them through. Finally you can use ready-dried mushrooms like porcinis, which again are brought to life

with boiling water and a little marinating. The latter, though, can be a bit more expensive, so the choice is entirely yours.

4　Final step is to purée up the last ingredients – the onion and the garlic – with a pinch of salt and pepper and a splash of water and soy sauce to make a nice flavoursome paste to dollop at the top of your jar. The best way is either to use an electric or hand blender or a pestle and mortar. But, if all else fails, use a small bowl and the end of a rolling pin to pound it to a paste.

5　Your instant noodles are now ready to go. If you're saving for later pop the lid on and put in the fridge; if you just can't wait to get stuck in, pour over just enough boiling water to cover all the ingredients and let it sit for 3 minutes to marinate the lot together. Then give the whole lot a really good stir and leave to sit for another 3 minutes before giving it one final stir through, adding a final hit of salt, pepper or soy sauce if you think it needs it. Then scoff it down with a fork, taking care not to dribble the lovely curried juices down your chin too much.

'OH DEAR, I SEEM TO HAVE GOT A LITTLE PLASTERED . . .'

We can hardly write a chapter on the great and the good, in a book about British Army cooking without giving mention to the most famous British military movie meal of all time – the breaking of bread at the end of *Carry On up the Khyber*. For many people, this is the quintessential *Carry On* film, indeed it is the only one considered good enough to make it into the British Film Institute's Top 100 movies of all time (sneaking in at number 99). For those of you unfamiliar with the film, it ends in a quite brilliant scene where series regulars Sid James, Joan Simms and Charles Hawtrey, dressed in their finest finery, enjoy a formal dinner, serenaded by a string quartet as the building they are in is shot at, blown up and otherwise attacked by Kenneth Williams and Bernard Bresslaw. What's most fantastic about this set-up is the way the Brits continue to eat, drink and make small talk while the world around them,

literally, crumbles. Waiting staff are shot, violin players are blown up and the ceiling falls in and, yet, nothing can stop the bonhomie and passing of port. Joan Simms's line, which titles this entry, was entirely improvised after a big chunk of faux masonry got lodged in her hair from an over-zealous on-set special-effects guy. Talking of which, the stuff falling onto their plates was brick masonry dropped from a great height by men at the top of big ladders. The cast had been served cold ham and boiled potatoes to double up as the sumptuous meal and no one wanted to eat anything covered, as it was, in tonnes of dirt.

We would love to say this scene is based upon a real-life military meal but, sadly, it is simply a brilliant invention of the writer Talbot Rothwell. Rothwell wrote nineteen *Carry On* films as well as the TV series *Up Pompeii*, starring Frankie Howerd. Rothwell, himself, was no stranger to the British Forces, though,

being a pilot in the RAF who was shot down during WWII and made a prisoner of war. In fact, it was during his time in the stalag that he started writing. Also, athough the characters and scenes were fictional, the historical context of the film is entirely accurate. It is set in 1895, a year when British Forces fought two major battles against Afghan and Pashtun tribesman. The British Army in that area was also heavily represented by the kilt-wearing Gordon Highlanders, who mirror the film's 'skirted devils' of the Third Foot and Mouth Regiment. Coincidentally this all took place in the same geographical areas as our present-day troops find themselves in combat in Afghanistan.

So there you have it, a brief summary of what is, in our opinion, the most famous military movie meal of all time. I'll leave the last word to Sir Sidney Ruff-Diamond, played, of course, by the inimitable Sid James: 'What are we going to do? We're British. We won't do anything . . .'

JOE GRIFFIN'S CORNED BEEF FRITTERS AND NELSON'S TART

Joseph Bernard Griffin is a former telegraphist air gunner with 771 Squadron of the Fleet Air Arm – the branch of the Royal Navy responsible for the operation of naval aircraft – and was involved in the D-Day landings. During his time in the Navy he was honoured with the Silver Anti-Submarine and Silver Anti-Minesweeping Medal, the 1939/1945 Star, the Atlantic Star, the British Commonwealth Defence Medal and the Inter-Allied Victory Medal. He is also my granddad.

Joe, like an entire generation, was given no choice but to serve in the Armed Forces during World War II. He is a hero of mine for not just defending our country and the rest of Europe against the rise of Fascism but, also, as befits this book, someone who encouraged me to cook, by showing that 'real' men aren't out of place in the kitchen. One of my proudest moments was joining him and the surviving scant number of the TAGs

on Remembrance Sunday in the march past the Cenotaph. It was so humbling to be among what remains of this generation of men who served without question and with such honour. That day will stay with me forever. I don't include him in this chapter because his story is, by any means, unique or special – no doubt there are men and women in your own family who have similar experiences – and I encourage you to ask them about it before they are gone and it is too late – but he is here because he is very special to me and serves as just one example of a generation that gave so much. If I may, I'll let Granddad tell his own story.

'When I joined the Navy as a very naïve eighteen-year-old in July 1939, I was told by the recruiting officer that they were only taking in cooks and stewards but not to worry because, as soon as I got to the naval barracks in Portsmouth, I could transfer to

whichever branch I wanted. Not for the first time, I discovered the Navy could be economical with the truth! In January 1940 – fully qualified in scrubbing galley decks and peeling spuds – I found myself on the Fish Quay in Hartlepool, looking down onto the deck of a scruffy-looking ex-fishing trawler called the *Beb Dearg*, which had been converted into a minesweeper. There was a crew of twenty and, from the skipper to the stoker, they were all ex-fishermen, all apart from me, who was expected to supply them with three square meals a day. The galley was tiny – approximately 6 foot square – with a cast iron, coal- burning range covered in thick grease and choked with soot, and every inch of that 6 foot square was infested with cockroaches. I spent the next few days getting the place as clean as I could – the range didn't end up looking too bad and, at the very least, it worked – and the cockroaches and I came to an understanding: "Stay out of the way when I am around." I wasn't a happy bunny but you just got on with it.

'Our job was to keep the shipping lanes clear from Middlesbrough to Humber and, although we were attacked by enemy aircraft a few times and once nearly got blown up by acoustic mines, it was really very boring sweeping the same channel week after week. Towards the end of 1941, I heard they were asking for volunteers to train as telegraphist air gunners in the Fleet Air Arm and I jumped at the chance. After passing the very stringent medical and education tests, I began training at Worthy Down, Hampshire, which involved learning wireless and visual communications and radio maintenance, and quite a lot of flying in obsolete planes. The "gunnery" part of the training was just two weeks in St Merryn, Cornwall, where we learned about Lewis, Vickers, Browning and, even, Tommy guns – firing them at drogues towed by other planes.

> 66 The galley was tiny – approximately 6 foot square . . . and every inch of that 6 foot square was infested with cockroaches. 99

'After passing out, I joined 771 Squadron, which was a Fleet Requirements Unit stationed at Scapa Flow in Orkney – the main British naval base. The posting involved doing whatever was needed from towing targets to anti-submarine patrols. We were flying two or three times every day in a variety of planes. I, luckily, survived three "prangs" – the first involved the plane's engine failing at 1,000ft and plummeting into a ploughed field resulting in some minor head and leg injuries. A month later the exact same thing happened again but this time I knew what to expect and escaped relatively unscathed. The last saw my plane's brakes fail on landing, so we ran out of runway, overshot into a field and tipped right over – again, luckily, no injuries. Other TAGs, sadly, weren't so fortunate and we lost a few good men. In February 1944 all leave was suddenly cancelled. We were instructed to fly, virtually, around the clock in order that we could get the fleet ready for something – something "big".

That event turned out to be D-Day. After the invasion on 6 June 1944 our job was finished and, so, leave was restored and I finally got married to your Nan on June 17.'

The rest, as they say, is history.

As I said before, it is humbling to hear what people, like my granddad, did for us all, and only that generation of men could describe a life that included being routinely shot at by Luftwaffe, nearly being blown up and surviving three plane crashes as 'boring'!

So now to the matter in hand – food – and it is unsurprising that the Navy, being a 'salty breed', had some interesting thoughts on the subject. Some (rejected) suggestions my granddad made for his entry in this book included 'Shit on a Raft', which was the Navy's rather prosaic way of describing mushrooms on toast, and a dish of egg, sausage and chopped tomatoes called 'A Train Smash'. I have chosen, instead, the far more appetising-sounding Corned Beef Fritters followed by Nelson's Tart.

CORNED BEEF FRITTERS

For one to four servings

You will need:
1–2 large potatoes
110g plain flour
150ml milk or water
salt and pepper
1 can of corned beef
vegetable or sunflower oil for
    frying

How you do it:

1 Peel the potato and cut it into 5mm thick slices before boiling in a pan of salted water. When the spud slices have been in for about 5 minutes (you want them to be just cooked but still firm) fish them out with a slotted spoon and set to one side.

2 Next, whisk the flour and milk or water together to make a thick batter and season with salt and pepper.

3 Now heat a pan of oil for deep-frying. It's ready when tiny spoonful of

66 … someone who encouraged me to cook by showing that 'real' men aren't out of place in the kitchen. **99**

batter dropped in rises to the surface and sizzles furiously. Meanwhile, open up the corned beef and cut it into similar-sized 5mm slices before making up 'sandwiches' of beef between two slices of potato. Dip them in the batter, then gently lower them into the hot oil, and deep-fry for 3–4 minutes until golden brown and crisp on the outside and soft and tender inside. Delicious. The beauty of this dish – as my granddad pointed out – was that, with food shortages, nothing here was wasted. Any leftover spuds or corned beef were mixed and fried the next day to make corned beef hash.

NELSON'S TART

For four to eight servings

You will need:
1 sheet of ready-rolled shortcrust pastry
1 jar of red jam – strawberry or raspberry, ideally
400g can of custard

How you do it:

1   Preheat the oven to 200°C/gas 6. Line a shallow baking tin, about 28 x 18cm, with the sheet of shortcrust pastry. When it is all tucked in and pressed nicely into the corners, lay a sheet of greaseproof paper on top of the pastry and then on top of that add some dried peas, lentil or beans which will hold the pastry in place and prevent it puffing up when you cook it.

2   Place the lined pastry case in the oven and bake for 10 minutes. Take it out and remove the peas/lentils/beans and greaseproof paper and pop the flan back in the oven for 5 minutes to just firm up the bottom.

3   When the pastry is baked, turn down the oven to 180°C/gas 4. Spread over a big thick layer of the jam and then top that with a layer of custard and bake in the oven until the custard sets. You want it to be slightly wobbly, not baked solid and rubbery, so check every 5 minutes or so. Remove from the oven, cool slightly, then cut into squares and serve.

CHAPTER 5

Wellingtons, Messes and Alcoholic Jam

Like all major fighting forces the world over, the British Armed Forces are divided into the 'Rank' and 'File' between those with stripes on their upper arms and those without. This division continues beyond the mess hall door. The food that is served up to the generals, admirals and wing commanders is just a smidge more special than that doled out to the squaddies, as you'll discover in this final chapter, with authentic, military recipes for Lobster Soufflé, Kedgeree and Beef, Oyster and Ale Pie.

LOBSTER SOUFFLÉ

This chapter is all about the food officers have been served down the years, and it not only proves that the 'Rank' get way better grub than the 'File', but also gives us a chance to stretch our cooking muscles a bit. These dishes are slightly more advanced either in terms of the number of ingredients or in the steps it takes to cook them, or purely in terms of how posh they sound – but don't let any of that put you off. As before, we have kept the instructions and ingredients to a minimum without sacrificing how tasty and, more importantly, how impressive the dish looks when you plate it up. As with all the best things in life, these recipes will produce the maximum impact with the minimum of effort.

A lobster soufflé, then, is a good place to start. Sounds fancy, has fancy ingredients but – with this recipe – is surprisingly easy to do and will snap knicker (or boxer) elastic from twenty paces. The dish was embraced by military chefs cooking in the officers' mess as a two-fingered salute to the various enemies who had nicknamed our top brass 'lobsters' due to their red uniforms. At least this means the dish sounds appetising, for the other nickname bestowed upon our officers was 'bloody backs' due to both the colour of the uniform and the widespread use of flogging as a means of punishment. 'Bloody Back Soufflé' anyone?

No, didn't think so . . .

> **"** As with all the best things in life, these recipes will produce the maximum impact with the minimum of effort. **"**

For four servings

You will need:

1 lobster, or 200g pack of pre-cooked and de-shelled lobster meat (or you could use 2 x 170g cans of white crabmeat, drained, instead)
50g butter plus a wee bit more for greasing and mixing with the lobster meat
50g plain flour
300ml milk
1 teaspoon English mustard
4 eggs
salt and pepper (preferably freshly ground)
chives

How you do it:

1 Begin by dismantling the lobster, if using a fresh cooked one. Now if you have chosen to go the pre-packaged variety – which is easier – you can obviously skip this step. (We also assume you haven't picked up a live lobster that needs boiling, but one that has been pre-cooked.) The easiest way is to pull off the claws and legs. Twist the upper pincer from the lower one and immediately some meat comes with it. Then grab a rolling pin, or a similarly weighty item, and bash open the shell on the remaining claw and scrape out the meat that's inside. Do the same with the other big claw and the legs but be warned, you won't get much meat out of the spindly ones. Don't worry, this is the only fiddly, time-consuming bit. Split the body in half. Remove the gills from behind the head and the dark vein that runs all down the length of the body. Now remove the meat from the tail. This is easy as it's just a case of scooping out what's in there. Put all the meat you excavate into a bowl and set it aside.

2 That's the lobster sorted. Now move on to the soufflé part of the dish. Start by rubbing butter all around the inside of a deep, straight-sided 15–18cm diameter dish (you can go smaller if you wish – just divide the mixture into 4 ramekin dishes). This is to ensure that the soufflé doesn't stick when it rises.

3 Next, grab the rest of the butter and melt it over a medium heat in a saucepan. Stir in the flour and mustard and keep it moving for about a minute.

Now, take the pan off the heat before gradually adding the milk a little at a time. Keep stirring as you add. Milk all in, pop the pan back on the heat and, using a whisk, keep the sauce moving until it is nice and thick and smooth – this should take several minutes (your muscles will thank you later). When thick and glossy, remove from the heat and allow it to sit on the side and cool.

4 Now preheat the oven to 200°C/gas 6 and get started on the eggs. First, separate the egg whites from the yolks, and the easiest way to do this is to crack the egg on the edge of a clean, grease-free bowl and gently pour the yolk from one half of shell to the other, so that the egg white drips into the bowl and you are eventually left with the yolk sitting in the eggshell. Do this with all four eggs and beat them thoroughly into the cooling sauce.

5 Back to the whites; season them well with a good pinch of salt and a grinding of black pepper and then grab a new clean whisk and start beating the living daylights out them. Keep going until the egg whites start to stiffen – and actually go 'white' from their starting translucent colour – and form stiff peaks (an electric whisk will make life a lot easier if you have one).

6 Next comes the trickiest bit of the recipe and the key to making the soufflé rise (or fail and fall). Take a metal spoon and gently mix the whipped-up whites into the sauce. What you are aiming to do is 'fold' the whites in and not stir them into oblivion, so use a light figure-of-eight movement, gently rotating the spoon with a turn of the wrist as it gently cuts and turns the mixture. (The reason being that the whites, due to your excellent whisking, contain a lot of air and are plumped up to form all those lovely peaks, which must not be knocked out as this is the air that will expand when heated and make the soufflé rise when it is popped in the oven.)

7 Okay, now grab your buttered dish and drop in your lobster meat – if you can, mix the meat with a knob of melted butter – and then spoon the soufflé mixture on top of it – again be careful not to over-whisk it. When you pour the soufflé mix in, you want just enough in there so it sits above the rim of the bowl – don't worry about it spilling over as it should be 'stiff' enough to hold its shape. One final thing you can also do is to run a knife around the outside lip of the dish to guard against it sticking to it as it cooks and rises. Place your dish on a baking tray and pop into the oven and bake it for 25–30 minutes. Do not be tempted to open the oven before this time is up as the sudden change in temperature will mean your risen soufflé will sink like a stone. Keep an eye on it through the oven window and when it is risen and nice and golden on top – and ideally with a slight wobble to it still – take it out and serve immediately (again to minimise chance of collapse) with a sprinkling of chives on top.

ERECTION DESELECTION

Just like world-class athletes in training for their next big race, or boxers prepping for a big fight, soldiers, too, had to withhold from activities of an, ahem, 'intimate nature' in order to maintain focus on their upcoming operation. The main difference between the sportsmen and the squaddies though was that the soldiers had no idea that was what they were doing. As unbelievable as it sounds, it appears the ruling ranks of the armies of the world were, for many years, putting something in their soldiers' food to reduce their desire for a spot of horizontal jogging. In Britain in the two World Wars, it was bromide in the tea (of course it would be our national drink they would attack – the swine!). In France it was the rationed wine (again they knew our French friends wouldn't give that a miss). In Germany it was iodine in the coffee, and in the good old US of A it was said to be potassium nitrate – better known as saltpetre – into the breakfast eggs which did the trick. (Apparently, though, it was easy to spot as it gave the scrambled eggs a startlingly green tinge.)

As if going to war wasn't hard enough, this does seem particularly cruel and unusual punishment for the serving men and women, but clearly the officers, admirals and flight lieutenants had good reason to do so. Perhaps it was to focus the fighting force on the matters at hand, but the activity was as widespread as it was unwelcome. Of course the powers-that-be denied doing such a thing and suggested that there were other reasons why their soldiers displayed an inability to 'troop the colour'. One such suggestion being that spending the day being shouted at by scary, angry men while covered in mud, blood and your own tears is not many people's idea of a romantic scene-setting situation. They may have a point.

Any such doctoring of the food is, of course, a practice which is long gone. Quite apart from being almost certainly illegal, some of the substances that had been used turned out not to be quite what was hoped for. Saltpetre, for example, while being widely used for all manner of problems such as asthma and arthritis since the eighteenth century, fell out of favour somewhat when side effects such as excruciating kidney damage, dangerously high blood pressure and death were discovered. (Think it's fair to say that forcing such a substance on your troops is a bit extreme to stop a few bouts of morning glory.) So we think it's fair to say the present-day soldiers can be thankful for a lot more than improvements in their body armour, telecommunications and food.

KEDGEREE

Whilst the average squaddie has never had much to look forward to in the mornings – often being awoken by nearby shelling or screamed abuse from a sergeant major – the breakfast ritual of the colonial officers was far nicer. They would be gently brought round from their slumber by some lightly lilting classical music emanating from a wind-up gramophone, the sweet caress of a soothing breeze from the punkawallah's efforts swinging the giant ceiling fan back and forth, and from the ravishing aroma of a simmering pot of kedgeree tickling the nostrils. Kedgeree – as an Indian breakfast dish – can be traced back as far as the 1300s. It became popular in the Army not only for its tastiness but also because, before the advent of the fridge, it was a good way of using up yesterday's leftovers before they spoilt. There was a third reason it was particularly favoured by the officer class, and that was because it's supposed to be especially good at combating a hangover, which is, surely, a good enough reason to give it a go.

For six servings

You will need:
1 onion
50g butter
300g rice (ideally basmati)
1 teaspoon curry paste (korma or
    madras is good)
bunch of fresh coriander, chopped
200ml milk
100ml double cream
3 eggs
350g smoked haddock fillet (skinned
    and any bones pulled out)
salt and pepper
1 handful of fresh parsley, chopped

How you do it:
1   Start with the onion. As this is traditionally a breakfast dish, chop it up small as you don't want a really fierce hit of chunky onion first thing in the morning. (Well, *you* might, but your other half or colleagues may not thank you for the bad breath assault. Of course if you are aiming to have this at lunch or supper or you don't care what anyone else thinks – go for the thick option.) When your onion is the right size, fry it for a few minutes on a low to medium heat, in a knob of the butter. When the onion starts to go translucent, throw in the rice. Give the whole lot a good stir, and keep stirring

> **❝** . . . especially good at combating a hangover, which is, surely, a good enough reason to give it a go. **❞**

for a few minutes more so that the rice starts absorbing the flavours and, more importantly, doesn't stick to the bottom of your pan and burn.

2 After about 5 minutes add in your chosen teaspoon of curry paste – korma if you want a nice, gentle early-morning buzz, something like a madras if you want something with a bit more of a kick – and half of your chopped coriander (leaves and stalks) and stir through again. After a further few minutes of frying, add the milk, cream and 200ml water. What you'll notice straightaway is the dish slows right down in terms of cooking as you have gone from 'frying' to 'boiling', as adding in all that liquid has cooled the pan. So whack up the heat and get it bubbling away again.

3 At this point, in another saucepan, put some water on to boil, which we'll return to in a minute to boil the eggs. After the rice has simmered for a few minutes, add the fish (just break it up with your fingers into good-sized flakes) and stir it through. Now you need to keep returning to the dish, stirring it and

checking to see if the rice is cooked. If the kedgeree starts to dry out and the rice still isn't cooked, simply add in a spot more water. If it is too runny but the rice is done, take the pan off the heat, cover it with foil and let it sit for 5 minutes or so, and the excess should be absorbed before your very eyes.

4 While the rice is finishing off, gently drop your eggs into the boiling water, being careful not to crack the shells. Leave them to bubble away for 3 minutes or so if you want them runny and a little

longer – say 5 minutes – if you want them hard-boiled. Pop them into cold water to cool slightly, then carefully remove the shells.

5 To finish the dish off, season the curried rice with as much salt and pepper as you like and stir through the parsley. Then serve it up with the boiled eggs sliced or quartered on top, another sprinkle of the remaining chopped coriander and the remaining good knob of butter, which will melt and ooze through the whole lot.

CHICKEN MARENGO

This slightly unusual-sounding dish was said to be the favourite of none other than one Monsieur Napoleon Bonaparte. It was named after the Battle of Marengo, which took place in 1800 and saw Bonaparte's French Army defeat the Austrians. Once all hostilities had ceased, Napoleon turned to his personal chef – Dunand – and asked him to cook something suitably celebratory. Dunand, being an army chef and therefore unendingly resourceful and inventive, had a quick forage about to see what ingredients he could find. Of course, had this been the British Army of the 1800s, Napoleon would have soon been feasting on a dirt-clagged potato served on a bed of wilting knotweed and a side of dead rat and the dish probably wouldn't have made it into the book. However, our Gallic cousins have a bit more of a

flair for these sorts of things and the chef was soon knocking up Chicken Marengo after his search had turned up a chicken, some eggs, a tomato, an onion, some garlic, a handful of olives, a crayfish and a splash of cognac from NB's personal hip flask. The chef is even reported to have cut up the chicken using Napoleon's sabre (as I said, all about style, the French). Bonaparte liked it so much (and who wouldn't?) that he insisted the ingredients were never to be changed and he subsequently had it cooked before every battle he went into, believing it to be lucky.

While some might find it unpalatable to be including a dish from the French Military in a book about British Forces food, we feel it counts because a dish fit for Napoleon was obviously something that would soon be adopted by the British officers – and so it proved. It's a popular dish on the menu in many an officers' mess to this day, albeit without the crayfish or fried eggs (but feel free to add if you so desire).

For four servings

You will need:
4 chicken breasts – skin on if possible (or you can use leg portions, which are cheaper)
olive oil
salt and pepper (preferably freshly ground)
plain flour
1 tablespoon butter
3 large tomatoes, chopped
1 handful of black olives, with the stones removed
3 garlic cloves
250g button mushrooms
150ml white wine
200ml chicken stock, fresh or made with a stock cube
2 tablespoons of tomato purée or a 300g can of cream of tomato soup
fresh parsley, chopped
crusty bread

How you do it:

1 Start by seasoning the chicken breasts or thighs. Rub a little olive oil on them, sprinkle over some salt and black pepper and then give them a light dusting with flour. Heat a splash more olive oil in a frying pan, add the butter and let it melt before adding in the chicken and frying for a couple of minutes until it is nice and brown all over. Carefully take them out of the pan and set them on some kitchen paper to soak off any excess oil. (Don't worry, we're not about to give you salmonella. You haven't finished cooking them just yet – this was just to get things started and the skin good and crispy.)

2 Back to the pan, and now add in the chopped tomatoes, olives (whole or chopped is fine), the peeled and chopped garlic (or just give them a squeeze through a garlic press if you have one), the button mushrooms (no need to chop as they are so small, just wipe them over to remove any excess dirt), the white wine and the chicken stock. There's one final ingredient to go in depending on whether you want to be more authentically French (the tomato purée) or whether you want to 'British' it up a bit (the contents of a small can of tomato soup) – the choice is yours. When it is all in, bring it to the boil and then lower the heat to a nice blipping simmer, before adding your chicken back into the pan. Pop a lid on and let it cook away for 30–40 minutes until the chicken is really tender and cooked through. When the time is up, give it a taste and add in a little more salt or pepper if it needs it. When you're happy, plate a big spoonful of the dish up, starting with a chicken breast or thigh for each person, before ladling on a good dollop of the delicious sauce. Sprinkle each dish with some parsley and serve each plate with a big chunk of fresh bread, ideally fresh out of the oven.

BEEF WELLINGTON

It seems only right and proper to redress the balance somewhat, and follow the excellent, but unapologetically French, Chicken Marengo with something a little more patriotic. Step forward Beef Wellington – named after our naval hero the Duke of Wellington and as British as a wet Bank Holiday Monday. While there are many origins for this meal that don't involve Good Old Wellie, such as that the finished dish is so named because it resembles a brown, shiny wellington boot; it's named after the town it was invented in, Wellington, New Zealand; or it's not named after anything, just entirely invented in the 1960s, we choose to believe the legend that it was first cooked to commemorate the duke's victory at the Battle of Waterloo. (After all, a legend such as he deserves a little more for defeating Napoleon than just a song by ABBA.) This great dish is said to be made up of all of the duke's favourite ingredients and has made frequent appearances at officers' dinners ever since its inception. In fact to this very day the Queen's Lancashire Regiment annually celebrate the duke's victory with a bit of a parade and then dinner in the officers' mess where this is the main event.

This is one of those recipes that can put people off simply because of their reputation for being a bit posh. Well, fear not. We have reduced the ingredients and instructions to their simplest form but can promise you something that still tastes great and looks like you've been slaving over it for days.

> ❝ Beef Wellington – named after our naval hero the Duke of Wellington and as British as a wet Bank Holiday Monday. ❞

For four servings

You will need:
1 kg piece of beef fillet
olive oil
salt and pepper (preferably freshly ground)
15 slices of prosciutto
250g pâté (ideally mushroom)
500g ready-to-roll puff pastry
plain flour
2 egg yolks, beaten together with 2 teaspoons water
gravy (laced with a little port or red wine, if liked) and vegetables, to serve

How you do it:

1 Begin by preheating the oven to 200°C/gas 6 and while it is warming, pop the beef fillet into a foil-lined roasting tray. Now beef fillet is expensive, especially at this size and weight (but is the best and will give you melting tenderness), so you could go for a lesser but still good-quality long, narrow, roasting joint. Basically, get the best piece you can afford without having to sell one of your kidneys – the dish will still be a cracker. Rub the beef all over with some olive oil and crack over some fresh black pepper and salt.

2 When the oven is up to temperature, bung the beef in for 15–20 minutes. Don't worry if the meat still looks a little too rare for your taste, it will be cooked again later, but we're aiming for a medium-rare pinkness to the beef when it's finished. Feel free, then, to cook for longer or shorter to suit your taste. When the time has elapsed, remove the meat from the oven and let it cool before popping into the fridge for 20 minutes.

Switch off the oven because you won't need it for ages.

3 While the meat is cooling, tear off two large pieces of clingfilm and overlap them on a big chopping board or on a suitably large kitchen surface or table. Now position the 15 slices of prosciutto (for the uninitiated, fancy dried-out Italian ham) on the clingfilm in two slightly overlapping rows. Next, spread half the pâté all over the rows of prosciutto; mushroom is best for the dish, though you can use whatever flavour you like. (A fancy version of mushroom pâté – a 'duxelle'– is used in the dish when it's served in the kind of the restaurant that makes your wallet weep from just perusing the menu, but rather than spend hours reducing, cooking and blending mushrooms, this will do the job.)

4 That done, grab the, by now, cooled beef and sit it on top of the pâté.

Spread the remainder of the pâté on the top of the meat. Next, very carefully draw up the clingfilm and wrap the beef in it. When it is covered in the film, gently roll it around so that the prosciutto encircles the meat and then shape the lot into a big fat sausage shape, twist the ends of the clingfilm to tighten it all together as you go. When it is done, pop it back in the fridge while you sort out the pastry.

5 Dust a little flour onto a work surface, a rolling pin and your hands (all to stop the pastry from sticking). Roll out the pastry until it would easily cover the prepared piece of beef (both length- and width-wise) with a bit to spare, and when you are ready, carefully unwrap the meat from the clingfilm and sit it in the centre of the pastry. Don't worry if bits of pâté or prosciutto come free, just patch and mend as you go and the pastry will cover most of your sins. When it is in place, brush all round the edge of the pastry with a little of the beaten egg yolks. Carefully lift the long edge of the pastry that is furthest away from you and lay it over the meat, repeat with the end closest to you so the pastry overlaps and press gently to seal. Next, turn the whole thing over and tuck the 'ends' underneath the Wellington. Turn it back over again before putting it on a plate and popping it one last time in the fridge to chill and rest for at least 40 minutes (though you can leave it for as long as 24 hours).

6 Finally, when you can take it no more, and need to get to the eating stage, crank the oven up to 200°C/ gas 6 and brush the whole lot over thoroughly with the remaining beaten egg yolks (this will turn the pastry golden brown when it is cooked) and cook it for 20–25 minutes until puffed and golden brown. Let it rest a few minutes before carving into nice big thick slices and serving it with some boozy gravy and vegetables.

HOW THE ARMY INVENTED CURRY

We men like a good curry. Like salmon who once a year have no choice but to swim upstream to spawn, so men the length and breadth of Britain subconsciously head for their favourite curry houses every Friday and Saturday night. (And, if God hadn't invented the female disapproval gene, we'd also be there Sundays, Mondays, Tuesdays . . .) But next time you are about to tuck into a chicken tikka masala, prawn rogan josh or lamb vindaloo ponder this – you wouldn't be doing so if it weren't for the officers of the British Army.

The story begins back in the 1700s when some 20,000 British soldiers were first stationed across India. (From that point on, the numbers of soldiers stationed there continued to grow so that by the time WWI rolled around most British regiments had a battalion stationed in Asia.) While there, the officers in particular were served the local recipes – albeit ones adapted to mellow out the spicy ingredients – by the local cooks sequestered into the Army ranks. The British came to name this new food as 'curry' even though it would have been a whole heap of different things – madras, rogan josh, dopiaza and so on. The word 'curry' is most probably a British mangling of the Tamil word 'khari', which means 'sauce' or 'gravy', which we presume they would have heard the locals use when talking about this new, wonderful food they were being cooked. The word 'curry' became so widely used around this time that the local Indian chefs and civilians started calling their dishes that when serving it to the British.

Over time, the British in India became so accustomed to curry that it became part of their day-to-day diet. The brigadiers and generals enjoyed curries packed with fresh meat, fruit and veg – the likes of mango, banana, coconut, tomato and onion – all topped off with previously unheard-of spices like cumin, turmeric and coriander. (Throw in a stiff gin and tonic and a cigar and they were all set.) The Forces chefs eventually began serving curries to enlisted men, too, as the new dish not only kept up morale but also meant that the meat rations would last longer. Sunday's roast beef became Monday's cottage pie became Tuesday's curry.

On their return to Britain, these privates and generals alike all craved the spicy dish and so Forces chefs here continued to cook up a curry. From there the dish started being prepared at home by loving wives and the rest is glorious, spicy history.

The surviving manuals of army catering show that while a curry was always on the menu the ingredients have changed over time. The basic 1904 curry was just curry powder added to beef stew (beef, onions and vegetables) but, by 1939, apple, coconut and bay leaves were included. In the 1950s, tomato purée and chutney were introduced and, today, a British soldier's ration packs aren't complete without a balti chicken or lamb madras and every mess hall has a widely cherished 'curry night'.

So there you have it: our national obsession with curry wouldn't have happened without the Army – perhaps we should all say a little 'thank you' the next time we're about to tuck into a takeaway.

ORIENTAL PORK

Superglue, the microwave, sat navs – three everyday things we all take for granted, that were invented by the Armed Forces. (Superglue was used to seal battle wounds, the microwave was a side effect of radar and sat navs exist because of GPS – global positioning system – that was used for navigation and finding the enemy so we could, more accurately, bomb the living daylights out of them.) Well, to that fine list we can add Chinese food. Following the British Armed Forces victories over China in the Opium Wars during the mid to late 1800s, the first wave of Chinese immigrants began to arrive in this country, bringing with them their awesome cuisine. This, combined with our officers stationed in the Far East (we had British Forces not only in China but also Malaysia and Hong Kong) being served local food and loving it before returning home, meant that there was soon an eager audience for the food. Across the port cities of Liverpool, Cardiff and London, Chinese families would set themselves up in restaurants to first serve their community and then the growing number of returning soldiers. As with everything, it was the ranked men who got served the best grub while 'in country' and took to it first. They were also the wealthiest and, therefore, could afford to hire cooks back home or take advantage of the various restaurants springing up. Hence the reason dishes like this popped up on the majors', captains' and admirals' tables. Over time – just like curry – the likes of Oriental Pork became more commonplace and open to all. Thank goodness for that.

For four servings

You will need:

1 green pepper

2 onions

1 spring onion

125g shiitake mushrooms (or use 'normal' white ones)

200g pak choi (or spinach)

1 red chilli

1 garlic clove

1 thumb-sized piece of fresh ginger

2 tablespoons sesame oil (or olive or sunflower oil)

25g butter

4 boneless pork steaks

salt and pepper (preferably freshly ground)

4 tablespoons tomato ketchup

2 tablespoons red-wine vinegar

1 tablespoon Worcestershire Sauce

dark soy sauce

1 tablespoon clear honey

75ml chicken stock (fresh or made with ¼ stock cube)

300g egg noodles

1 handful of fresh coriander

1 lime

How you do it:

1 Start by preparing the veg. Cut off the stalk and remove the seeds from the green pepper, then chop it up. Peel and chop up the onions and the spring onion (though save some of the latter back for a bit of fancy garnish later). Next, wipe and thickly slice the shiitake mushrooms (despite their unusual name, they are quite easy to get hold of these days). Trim and thickly slice the pak choi into shreds. Put to one side in neat piles.

2 Now chop up the red chilli (leave the seeds in if you like extra heat), peel and finely slice the garlic (or just crush it with a garlic press) and peel and grate the ginger. Heat the oil and butter in a large saucepan (or wok if you have one – either will do), and if you can get it, use sesame oil as it adds a nice, authentic toasted nut taste to your dish. While it's heating rub some salt and pepper onto both sides of the pork, before slicing it up into strips.

3 Next, drop the chilli, garlic and ginger into the hot oil and butter and stir round for a minute or so.

4 Now add the pork strips to the fragrant oil and butter. Keep the pork moving around for 5–6 minutes, to ensure it both cooks through and doesn't stick and burn. Now chuck in the onions you prepared earlier and stir-fry them for a couple more minutes. Now chuck in the rest of the prepared veg and cook for a few more minutes until softening but still with a bit of crunch.

5 Before you start on the tasty sauce, get a pan of salted water on to boil for the noodles. Now add the tomato ketchup, red-wine vinegar, Worcestershire sauce, a good splash of soy sauce and the honey to the pork mixture and give the lot a damn good stirring. Finally, add in the chicken stock and stir once more. Simmer on a low heat for a few minutes and adjust the taste with a little more soy sauce if you think it needs it.

6 While this blips away, drop the noodles into the boiling water. If they are fresh egg noodles then just a minute will do; if you are using a dried option then they will need a little longer, say 3–4 minutes (check the packet directions). When the noodles are done, drain them and drop them into the stir-fry and give the whole lot one last stir, before plating up and garnishing with some chopped fresh coriander (leaves and chopped stalk), the reserved bit of spring onion, a little squeeze of lime and another splash of soy sauce. Break open your chopsticks and get stuck in.

WHERE OFFICERS ARE MADE

Each of the three branches of the British Armed Forces – the Army, the Royal Navy and the Royal Air Force – has its own officer-training establishments.

Starting with the Army, it does its schooling, as has been previously mentioned, at the Sandhurst Royal Military Academy in Surrey. All British Army officers are trained here, as are a select few from invited foreign fighting forces. You cannot pay to get into the academy: every man and woman trained here is selected by the Army Officer Selection Board as having 'officer potential'. Training lasts just shy of a year (forty-eight weeks) and some of the great and good to have passed through its doors include both Princes William and Harry, as well as Churchill; Bond creator Ian Fleming; tune warbler James Blunt; and, as befits this book, perma-sozzled but, sadly, no-longer-with-us chef Keith Floyd.

The Britannia Royal Naval College is, as the name suggest, the Royal Navy's equivalent. The college is in Devon and the Navy has been training its best here since the 1800s. Entry is by application, though each potential officer is grilled by the Admiralty Interview Board, before having to pass a number of written aptitude tests and passing a strenuous physical fitness course. Again, training lasts just under a year (forty-nine weeks) and alumni of the college include many of our royal family. Prince William went there (though, to be fair to him, he underwent training in all three of the Armed Forces), as did Prince Charles and Prince Andrew, and Prince Philip. In fact it was here that he first clapped eyes on the young Princess Liz.

Finally, the Royal Air Force College, Cranwell, in Lincolnshire, the home of the best of the best of the RAF. The most recent of the three establishments, it only began life in 1919 when it became the world's first Air Force academy. The college also has the shortest course at just thirty-two weeks before cadets are commissioned. Just like a real life *Top Gun*, training includes classes in leadership, ethics and air-combat strategy. The likes of Prince William (him again), the man who invented jet propulsion, Sir Frank Whittle, and flying ace Sir Douglas Bader all passed through its doors.

ETON MESS

Eton Mess is a dish that was invented at – you guessed it – Eton and has been around since the 1800s when it was first served at the annual cricket game between Eton and Winchester College. There is another story that suggests it came about after a playful puppy was let loose at a picnic and smashed all the dishes' ingredients together. However, while we may never know exactly how it started, we do know it tastes good and that's all that matters. Of course, over the six centuries of its illustrious history, Eton has given the British Forces more than their fair share of field marshals, lieutenant colonels and brigadier generals, so it's no stretch of the imagination to see how this dessert would have been a staple dish of officers' mess halls down the years. Don't be put off by its slightly stuffy start in life, Eton Mess is really easy to make and tastes absolutely fantastic.

For four servings

You will need:
450g strawberries
4 tbsp kirsch or any other cherry
   liqueur or cherry brandy
330ml double or whipping cream
6 small meringue nests, crushed

How you do it:
1   Chop the strawberries up however you like (after first removing their stalks), place them in a bowl and pour over the kirsch. If you are in a hurry then crack on with the recipe if you have time, however, let the strawberries macerate in the booze for 2 hours.
2   Next, whip the cream until it stands in soft peaks. Then, when you are ready to eat, gently fold the sozzled strawberries and the smashed-up meringues into the cream. Grab the dishes you are going to serve it in, pile in the Eton Mess and attack with a spoon.

LAMB KEBABS

Officers' food isn't always about the 'fancy' dishes – though, as you've seen in this chapter already, there are plenty of those to go round. Take lamb kebabs, for instance. Regularly on the menus of mess halls across the globe, there isn't a soldier serving today who would pass up the opportunity to get stuck into one of these given half the chance. However, though the dish itself isn't swanky, the difference between the one the squaddies get and the one the officers tuck into is quite remarkable. The former would be an inspired blending of the basic compo rations served in a pitta bread and a dish made to as closely as possible resemble a kebab bought from a street van. The officers' kebab – as you will see – is packed full of cracking ingredients, exceptionally tasty and a more 'authentic' version of the dish. So if you've only ever eaten these after they've been carved from a big rotating stick in a greasy takeaway after closing time, gird your loins, get down the supermarket and prepare yourself. You're in for a real treat.

For four servings

You will need:
450g lean minced lamb
1 handful of fresh coriander, chopped
1 tablespoon garam masala
1 tablespoon ground cumin
2 garlic cloves (the Forces use ½ teaspoon garlic powder)
½ teaspoon ground ginger
1½ teaspoon ground cinnamon
chilli powder
salt and pepper

For the tzatziki:
150ml Greek-style or other plain yoghurt
5cm piece cucumber, peeled and grated
1 teaspoon dried mint

> **"** The officers' kebab . . . is packed full of cracking ingredients, exceptionally tasty and a more 'authentic' version of the dish. **"**

How you do it:

1 Put the lamb in a large bowl, then throw in everything else apart from the tzatziki ingredients, seasoning well with salt and pepper. Mix it with your hands, squeezing and squelching it until the lovely flavours are all mingled through the meat.

2 Once everything is blended together, divide it into four equal amounts before moulding each into a sausage shape.

3 Now you have a choice of how to cook them. The lazy way is to place your kebabs onto a baking tray and put the lot into the preheated oven at 190°C/ gas 5 and bake them for 15 minutes.

Or, for a more authentic kebab experience, you can mould each of the sausage shapes around a metal skewer and then either barbecue them or place them under a hot grill for a similar amount of time. You need to make sure you turn them every few minutes to ensure they cook evenly.

4 You can either serve them with plain yoghurt or with tzatziki. Simply put the yoghurt in a bowl. Squeeze the grated cucumber to make sure all that excess moisture is removed before stirring it in and adding the dried mint and some salt and pepper. Eat the kebabs hot, with the bowl of yoghurt or tzatziki to dip them into.

WHISKY MARMALADE

What better way to start the day than with a breakfast spread laced with hard liquor? As you would suspect, this kind of refined dining is reserved for the officer class – every one of their mess halls simply must have a pot of freshly made whisky marmalade to spread on their toast, muffins or crumpets. At the opposite end of the spectrum, most squaddies have to make do with 'hash' for breakfast – no, not in the Bob Marley sense of the word: this hash is a sticky combination of biscuits, margarine and jam from their twenty-four-hour ration packs, all smashed together in their mess tin and scoffed with the eyes closed. (We're reliably informed, while it looks like something a dog would bring up after eating a family-sized arctic roll, it actually tastes pretty good.) Back to this recipe, though, and what's brilliant about it is how the officers' chefs have improved upon something that was already considered a classic – by spiking it with huge amounts of booze. A fine idea and one that we feel should be extended beyond this particular recipe: gin porridge, muesli and Campari, or tequila Pop-Tarts anyone?

Makes about 1.5kg (3 large jars)

You will need:

1.5kg oranges (Sevilles are best for a bitter marmalade but ordinary sweet ones will do)
3 litres water
2 lemons
3kg granulated sugar
5 tablespoons whisky

How you do it:

1   Start by finding a large saucepan. Think big – humungous, even. It's got to hold all those oranges and three litres of water right from the off, so get rummaging around the back of the kitchen cupboards for something suitable. (Of course if you can't find one, and don't want to shell out on a brand-new bit of kit, then just halve all the above ingredients and use a smaller pan.) With suitable receptacle to the fore, put the oranges, the water and the juice from your lemons in and bring the whole lot to the boil. When it is bubbling away, turn the heat down to a slow simmer, cover the pan, and leave it to blip away for 2½ hours. (We know it's a long time but good things come to those who wait – perhaps you can do a little taste test on some whiskies to while away the time and find out the most suitable brand?).

2   When the time has elapsed, and presuming you haven't fallen asleep in a boozy haze, turn the heat right down and scoop out the, by now, very soft oranges, using a slotted spoon, and put them into a large bowl (but keep the water on the hob as you are going to use it again in a moment). When the oranges are cool enough to handle, chop them in half and scoop their insides out, dropping all the fleshy goodness back into the pan of water to simmer away for another 30 minutes. You may think it weird to be putting the pips and piths back in as well as the fruit but fear not – you're going to sieve them away at the end, and these bits and bobs (along with the lemon juice) help provide the dish with pectin, which is essential for getting the marmalade to set. (See page 108 and the recipe for Fruit Jelly for more on the magic of pectin if you are so inclined.) While it's bubbling away again, you have a choice to make about the peel. If you like to have a bit of it in your marmalade, then chop as much of it as you like into thin strips with a sharp knife and pop to one side; if you prefer it smooth then chuck it away.

3 When the 30 minutes is up, you need to pass all the contents of the pan through a sieve, into a second pan underneath, pressing and squeezing and squashing as much of the fruit and pulp through it as you can, to make a lovely thick juice (which will form the basis of your marmalade). When it's all been squashed through, add in the peel (if you choose to) and all the sugar and slowly bring this second pan to the boil, stirring constantly as you go to dissolve the lot.

4 When it feels as if all the sugar has melted – it should feel 'smoother' than before – whack the heat up and get it boiling away like crazy. This final blast on the hob is there to get the marmalade to set, but keep stirring while you heat it up, so that it doesn't stick to the bottom of the pan and burn. The process of getting it to set should take between 5 and 10 minutes and people who do this sort of thing all the time say you can tell if it's ready by dropping a blob of it on a very cold saucer or plate. If you push your finger through it, it should wrinkle up. If it spreads out like liquid, it's not ready. Alternatively, lift a wooden spoonful up out of the pot, tilt the spoon and let the marmalade run off back into the pan. If the last drop hangs suspended from the spoon in a jelly-like blob, it is ready. If not, keep bubbling away and check every minute or so until it is. Finally, and most importantly, the booze. Take the marmalade off the heat, stir in the whisky and leave the lot to cool for 10 minutes or so before emptying into sterilised jars (see page 146 and Johnson Beharry's noodle recipe for how to do this at home). Cover and label it and leave until cold and set. Your boozy breakfast spread is now ready to be employed as a little morning pick-me-up for months to come.

POACHER'S SOUP

Poacher's Soup is one of those 'does exactly what it says on the tin' recipes. It was invented by poachers with whatever they could get their hands on – hare and partridge, for instance – all cooked up with some veg. Now it's no surprise to discover that most of the ingredients that (illegally) went in the pot would have come from the grounds of the chaps who make up a large proportion of the officer class (no strangers themselves, of course, to shooting anything that moved on their land). These *Downton Abbey* sorts, therefore, did some stealing of their own

and 'nicked' the recipe from the poaching brigade but, obviously, used their own quail, pheasant or grouse. The dish then followed the promoted men around the world but the ingredients changed, depending on where they were stationed, ensuring more exotic wildlife – like a short-tailed bandicoot rat (Afghanistan) or perhaps a swarthy gerbil (Iraq) – found their way into the pot.

The beauty of this dish for us is, not only is it super-tasty but also you don't have to risk getting your backside peppered with buckshot while collecting your ingredients. Unless of course

your local Tesco is *really* dangerous, in which case you might want to consider moving house . . .

For four servings

You will need:
splash of olive oil
1 tablespoon butter
1 large onion
175g of prepared game meat (pheasant, hare, grouse, partridge or whatever else you fancy, or a pack of diced mixed game meat)
250g smoked bacon
2 garlic cloves
2 carrots
100g mushrooms
1 sprig of fresh thyme
25g plain flour
900ml beef or chicken stock
250ml red wine
1 teaspoon lemon juice
salt and pepper
chunks of fresh bread and butter, to serve

> ❝ Poacher's Soup is one of those 'does exactly what it says on the tin' recipes. ❞

How you do it:

1 Start by heating the olive oil and butter in as large a pot as you have a lid for. While the butter is melting, peel and chop the onion – it doesn't have to be finely chopped, and every chunk doesn't have to be the same size as this is more of a stick-to-your-ribs-warm-you-up-in-winter-type recipe – and bung it in.

2 When the onion has softened a bit but not started changing colour, it's on to the game. We're assuming you have bought ready-prepared meat and don't need to skin, nor remove any shotgun pellets from anything, so go ahead and place it all into the pan with the onions, and just brown it to get the cooking started, (you'll give it another blast in the oven later). When the game has browned all over, fish it out of the pot with a slotted spoon and place it to one side to cool.

3 Now cut up the bacon (snipping it into strips with a pair of clean scissors is by far the easiest way to do this). Add it to the lovely, by now golden, onion and the meat juice, and give it a good stir round. While the bacon begins to cook, (2–3 minutes should be enough time) peel and chop the garlic and carrots. Slice the mushrooms and chop the thyme. Add them all to the pot and give the lot a stir. With all that coated in the lovely oil/butter/meat juice combo, add in the flour to thicken things up a bit and mix well again. Let it bump along for a few more minutes and then gradually add the stock and wine.

4 Next put the browned game back in and whack up the heat to get it boiling. Once it is blipping away, turn the heat right down to a gentle simmer and pop a lid on the pot and then let it cook for 30 minutes. This should make the meat nice and tender and get all those lovely flavours mixing and blending. Check on it every 5–10 minutes to make sure it isn't drying out – if it is, add a splash of water – and give it a further gentle stir.

> **"**The beauty of this dish for us is, not only is it super-tasty but also you don't have to risk getting your backside peppered with buckshot while collecting your ingredients.**"**

5   Now because some game is quite fatty, sometimes when it is boiling away you will notice said fat collects on the surface of the soup. It's perfectly harmless but most people choose to skim it off. If you want to, then feel free, and there are all manner of ways of doing so, from the obvious – a spoon to ladle it off or some kitchen paper to blot it – to the more inventive but no less effective – a slice of bread or a cold lettuce leaf. As they used to say on *Blind Date*, 'The choice is yours.' (Readers under 20 years of age should consult with a responsible adult to find out what the heck we're talking about.)

6   When everything is soft and tender, take the soup off the heat and give the whole lot a blending. Now this is most easily done with a hand blender straight in the pot you are cooking in. Failing that, you can pour the soup into a food processor and blitz it. If you own neither then use a potato masher to mix together all the ingredients in the pot – be warned, though: doing it this way will take some time to achieve a good, thick, soupy consistency. When that's done, return the lot back to the heat and get it simmering away one final time while you add in the final ingredients – the lemon juice and, if you think it needs it, some salt and pepper. When you are happy with the taste, serve the soup up in big steaming bowls with chunks of freshly buttered bread.

ARE YOU OFFICER MATERIAL?

As we mentioned earlier in this chapter, any potential Army officer has to undergo nearly a year's worth of training at Sandhurst before being given their first commission. But before any of that can happen – before they can even set foot inside the academy – they have to pass a series of stringent tests and exams. Here is a list of them, so see if you have what it takes. You must be able to:

- Complete the infamous Sandhurst assault course, obstacles on which include a 2m-high rope climb, two long jumps to negotiate and a leisurely hop up some steps while carrying a log – and all in under three minutes.

- Do 44 press-ups in two minutes PLUS fifty sit-ups – also in two minutes.

- Do 10.2 on a shuttle-run beep test, which is the equivalent of running 2.5km in ten minutes.

- Complete a series of lengthy mental-aptitude tests which include verbal, numerical and abstract reasoning.

- Complete a series of 'Leaderless' tasks, in groups of six or eight, where you have to work out how to get a 'burden' (usually an oil drum or box of sand) between two points using planks, poles and ropes without it touching the floor. And all against the clock.

- Complete a series of theoretical planning exercises.

- And finally, partake in a series of group discussions on current affairs.

BEEF, OYSTER AND ALE PIE

Finest steak, posh oysters and booze. With those ingredients you know this will have been served to officers rather than squaddies over the years – especially when you further peruse the ingredients list and spot not one, but two, types of alcohol in it. We couldn't think of a better recipe to sign off on.

This dish was invented during the Victorian Era – a time when we had, effectively, gone to war with, and subsequently ended up owning, half the world. Indeed, it was a time when the British Empire was the largest the planet would ever see, and a time when our military superiority was unchallenged around the globe. A time that came to be known as the Pax Britannica – or British Peace – when our Navy was so good it was said to be better than the next two best navies combined. We controlled all of the key maritime routes, which brought in goods and food from all over the world. So this dish was a bit of a celebratory affair – a watch-out-Johnny-Foreigner-we're-here-to-kick-arse-take-names-and-eat-pie type of dish. While that time has clearly passed, this cracking recipe lives on, so get cooking and get a taste of what it felt like to rule the world.

For four to six servings

You will need:
splash of olive oil
675g stewing steak
5 shallots
1 tablespoon butter
250g smoked bacon
2 carrots
100g button mushrooms
2 garlic cloves
1 sprig of fresh thyme or ½–1 teaspoon dried
2 x 330ml cans of Guinness (or any other beer)
250ml of red wine
salt and pepper to taste
4 tablespoons plain flour
8 oysters
375g ready-rolled puff pastry
1 egg, beaten
vegetables of your choice, to serve

How you do it:

1 Start by heating some olive oil in a large flameproof casserole (one that is going to safely take all the ingredients you have, but not so big that it won't fit into your oven at the end for a bit of pastry baking). While it is heating up, cut the stewing steak into good, bite-sized chunks, then throw it into the hot oil and keep it moving around for a few minutes until all sides are browned. With any kind of cheap cut, like stewing steak, you need to cook it for a long time to make sure it's nice and tender and to maximise the flavour (as opposed to a fillet steak which can be done in 3–4 minutes flat, for example), so we will cook it more later. For now, fish out the beef with a slotted spoon and set it to one side on a plate.

2 Now peel and chop the shallots. Chuck the butter into the casserole – with all that lovely, meaty cooking juice – and, when it has melted, add the shallots. Shallots are from the onion family and don't take long to cook – three to four minutes max.

3 Next, snip the bacon into strips with scissors (for ease) and chop the carrots. Add both to the pot with the button mushrooms (just wipe them over first, no chopping required) and a nice sprinkling of thyme (you'll need to 'pluck' the leaves from the stalk if using fresh). Let it cook for another 5 minutes, giving it a stir along the way, and then put the beef back in and pour in the beer. (No point messing about: buy a four-pack and enjoy the others while you create your culinary masterpiece.) You may need to crank up the heat a little as you have gone from 'frying' the ingredients to 'simmering' them, and, much like when driving up a steep hill you need to increase your acceleration to maintain your speed, so you need a bit more heat to keep things bubbling along at the same rate. (When you have a good blip going, you can always turn it down again.)

4 After the ingredients have simmered away for 5 minutes, crush the garlic cloves if you have a garlic press – if you don't, peel and finely chop them

> **❝** . . . this dish was a bit of a celebratory affair . . . **❞**

up instead – and add to the casserole with the red wine. Cover the pot, turn the heat right down and let it bump along for 1½ hours or until the meat is tender. Keep checking throughout and stirring it every so often, and if it looks like drying out you can always chuck in a little more wine, Guinness or, even, water if your booze supplies are running low.

5 When the beef is tender, blend the flour with a little water and stir in until thickened, then take the casserole off the heat, give it a little taste and, if you think it needs it, add in a little salt and pepper. It needs to cool a bit before topping with pastry or the pastry will go soggy and slide into the filling so pop it to one side.

6 Now tackle the oysters. Oysters are one of those foodstuffs that can put people off even when they've never tried them. Perhaps it's something to do with eating them raw. Well, this is a great introduction to the be-shelled beauties as they are going to be gently cooked (as you would with other shellfish like mussels or clams) and so, hopefully, take away that 'squeamish' factor. The key to cooking them is to not do it too long and not on too high a heat – do either and they will become rubbish and rubbery. Either ask your supermarket or fishmonger to 'shuck' them (open up the clam-like shell) or, if you fancy doing it yourself, hold one at a time

in a cloth, rounded shell down, insert the sharp point of a knife between the two shells near the hinge and twist firmly until the top one is prised open from the bottom, then twist it off. Now simply

> 66 Finest steak, posh oysters and booze . . . We couldn't think of a better recipe to sign off on. 99

add the oysters to the dish and give it a good stir.

7 Preheat the oven to 200°C/gas 6 and roll out the pastry. If it's big and wide enough to cover the casserole

straight out the packaging, great, but if it isn't, simply dust the work surface with a little plain flour and give the whole lot a rolling over with a pin until it is. If there's enough pastry, ideally cut a strip off it, dampen the circumference of the dish and stick the strip all round it. Brush it with water, then top with the remaining pastry sheet (this helps glue the pastry to the dish). Alternatively, you can simply place the pastry sheet over the dish, cut around the edge to remove any excess, then 'squish' the pastry to the casserole edge with your finger. If you are feeling artistic you could also 'crimp' the pastry around the edge with a fork. Finally, brush the beaten egg over the pastry, to give it a golden finish, and bake in the oven for 25–30 minutes until the pastry has risen and is lovely and golden. Serve with some nice vegetables of your choosing.

YOU'RE RANK OUT OF ORDER

With swift apologies for the terrible pun that titles this little section, we hereby supply you, the gentle reader, with a list of the ranks of the British Army to show any lowly privates out there what, one day, they could achieve:

1 Officer Cadet – the rank held during the initial training at Sandhurst.

2 Second Lieutenant – the first rank held after being 'commissioned', i.e. successfully negotiating their way out of Sandhurst. This rank tends to be held for two years, during which time they gain further training in the regiment they are now attached to. At this rank they can lead, and be responsible for, up to 30 soldiers.

3 Lieutenant – this rank is typically held for a further three years. Still only responsible for 30 men, lieutenants have the opportunity to gain specialised skills outside their assigned unit.

4 Captain – second-in-command to a group of up to 120 men. Captains are now big players in the Army, getting involved in tactics, decision-making and other such operations.

5 Major – this is a big one, taking eight to ten years of service to achieve. Majors will command groups of up to 120 officers and men, and are responsible for all their training and welfare.

6 Lieutenant Colonel – typically commanding up to 650 men, covering some four or five entire units. LCs are responsible for military capability and discipline as well as training and welfare. This is usually a two-year appointment.

7 Colonel – at this rank, these military men are unlikely to spend much time commanding in the field. Colonels, instead, are the principle advisers to those above them. Talking of which . . .

8 Brigadier – commands entire brigade of men, approximately 3,000 soldiers.

9 Major General – commands entire divisions, as well as working closely with the Academy at Sandhurst to make sure everything is tickety-boo. Also holds senior roles at the MOD.

10 Lieutenant General – commands entire corps both in the UK and overseas in the Commonwealth. Holds very senior staff roles in the MOD.

11 General – the top of the tree. Generals make up the most senior roles like Chief of Defence, Supreme Allied Commander and Commander in Chief of All Land Forces.

ACKNOWLEDGEMENTS

My first 'thank you' must go to my family. To my beautiful wife Shelley – thank you for all your love and support not just in the eighteen months it took to write this book but for all the years we have been together. I wouldn't be the man I am without you. I love you.

To my beautiful baby boy, George – you are absolutely the best thing in the history of the world, ever. I am so proud to be your 'Dada'. I cannot wait to see what adventures lie ahead of us. I love you, little man.

To my parents for all their love and support and for teaching me how to cook my first dish – I've come a long way since that toasted cheese-and-tomato sandwich. And, as I mentioned in Chapter 4, to my granddad, Joe Griffin, who served his country with humility and honour, who, along with my nan, raised a loving family and showed me that 'real men' know their way around the kitchen.

Next to my friend and agent, Humfrey Hunter – who knew that FHM lunch nearly twelve years ago would have led

to this? Thank you, mate, for getting me to write this book – you were absolutely right: I have loved every minute of it. Needless to say this book wouldn't exist without you: your advice and support have been invaluable. Think I owe you another slap-up meal now! Here's to the next one . . .

I am also extremely fortunate to have in my corner not just one of the best publishing houses in the world in Constable & Robinson, but also one of the great publishing directors in Andreas Campomar. I am extremely proud to be a small part of the English-speaking world's oldest independent publisher and through it to have been introduced to, and work with, the world's poshest-sounding man (!) Andreas, your enthusiasm from the outset about how good this book could be was infectious and your support and input along the way has been fantastic. That you also had the good grace to allow me a healthy extension to my deadline when my baby boy was born is testament, if any were needed, that

you are truly one of life's good guys. Thank you, sir.

I also owe a huge debt of thanks to the wonderful Gina Rozner, whom I met through the day job, got on famously with and who serendipitously turns out to be Andreas's partner. I know that you had a big part to play at the beginning in telling Andreas what a great book you thought this could be and what a fab writer and all-round good egg I was (two out of three eh?). Thank you, Gina, for your belief in me and the book. I would also like to thank four other members of the Constable & Robinson family. To Charlotte Macdonald, Carolyn Humphries, Angela Martin and Becca Allen, who cajoled, edited, primped and polished me ready for my unveiling to the outside world.

I would also like to say a quick 'thank you' to James Steen, a wonderful writer who graciously pointed me in the direction of Alexis Soyer and his amazing stove. Thank you, sir, for your kind words and generosity of ideas.

I am also extremely lucky to have received the generous input of a huge number of famous ex-servicemen who each took time out of his exceptionally busy life to donate a recipe for the book. It is a testament to their good character and to the high regard each still holds his time spent in the Forces, that they got involved with the book so readily. Of course to get to those celebrities you must go via their gatekeepers and, once again, I have been blessed to have found myself knocking on the doors of some truly wonderful PRs, agents and managers. I cannot be more grateful to you all for passing on my request to your clients when it would have been so much easier to put it in the bin. So in no particular order a huge debt of thanks to: Andy McNab and Laura Sherlock at Andy McNab Security; to Chris Ryan and Barbara Levy; Johnson Beharry and Jaine Brent at JJB Creative; Michael Morpurgo, Laura West and Veronique Baxter at David Higham; Josh Lewsey and Matt Jones at GamePlan Solutions; and Sir Ranulph Fiennes, Charlie Campbell and Maggie Philips at Ed Victor. Thank you!

Finally, to every single member of the British Armed Forces who are, even now, doing impossibly brave things in terrible places all over the world, I am humbled by the sacrifices you make and the hard yards you put in every single day. I – and all of us – owe you a debt of gratitude that can never be repaid and are so very, very proud of what you do and who you are. Thank you.

INDEX

PICTURE CREDITS

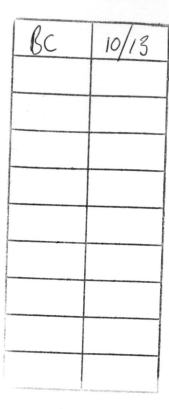

BC	10/13